Advance Praise for *Shanghai Demimondaine*

"This most intriguing book vividly evokes the glamour of Shanghai in its last period as one of the world's great cosmopolitan cities, while skilfully drawing together the threads of a complex and fascinating human story involving Japan China and the wider world."

—John Minford, Emeritus Professor of Chinese, ANU

"From sin to salvation to sin. Hordern tells the the fascinating life of "one of the most beautiful women" Emily Hahn had ever seen. Her life as paramour to an heir to the Japanese Shogun, high class prostitute in Shanghai, secret intelligence informer in Australia and finally to respectable woman back in Australia would almost be unbelievable if not true. A great read!"

—Douglas Clark, author of *Gunboat Justice*

"Unfolding like a detective story, Nick Hordern has tracked down the multiple lives of the unknown Lorraine Murray, who was born out of wedlock in morally censorious Australia. An exceptional beauty and unstable fabulist, she becomes the mistress of Prince Tokugawa, an elite prostitute in frenetic, war-torn 1930s Shanghai, the heroine of a novel by a New Yorker writer, then London society wife in a strange marriage. Extraordinary."

—Geoffrey Lehmann, winner of the Prime Minister's prize for poetry and author of *Leeward*

SHANGHAI DEMIMONDAINE

FROM SEX WORKER TO SOCIETY MATRON

NICK HORDERN

EARNSHAW BOOKS

Shanghai Demimondaine

By Nick Hordern

ISBN-13: 978-988-8843-04-6

BIOGRAPHY & AUTOBIOGRAPHY

Cover: Lorraine Murray by Edmund Toeg, c.1936

Author's photo by Graham McCarter

EB186

Published in Hong Kong by Earnshaw Books Ltd.

CONTENTS

Identities

Laurinna Agnes Treweek: name on Lorraine Murray's birth certificate, Adelaide, 22 January 1910

Lorraine Lee: name used by Lorraine Murray in Shanghai, 1933

Johnny Jean: Lorraine Murray's workname in Madam Louise's brothel, Shanghai, 1934–1936

Jean: non-fictional portrait of Lorraine Murray in Emily Hahn's 1944 memoir *China to Me*

Jill: fictional portrait of Lorraine Murray in Emily Hahn's 1947 novel *Miss Jill*

Lorraine: non-fictional portrait of Lorraine Murray in Emily Hahn's 1950 memoir *England to Me*

Dee Dee: Lorraine Murray's nickname for her patron Edmund Toeg; also the character of an ardent suitor in their fantasy relationship

Wunsy: Edmund Toeg's nickname for Lorraine Murray; also the character of a shy young girl in their fantasy relationship

Botchan: fictional portrait of Lorraine Murray's lover, the Japanese statesman Tokugawa Iemasa, in *Miss Jill*

The Shady Lady: nickname for Lorraine Murray used by Soviet agent Rupert Lockwood, 1954

Rainee: family nickname for Lorraine Murray, died Wagga Wagga, 6 January 2000

Prologue: At Farren's

... THE CABARETS are going full swing again. With the war business on, it seems to add a forced gaiety to it all ...

Australian businessman in Shanghai

One night in October 1937 the American writer Emily Hahn went out dancing to Shanghai's hottest jazz nightclub, Farren's. The Sino-Japanese War had broken out two months before and the besieging Japanese army was drawing closer: there were checkpoints on the roads and distant explosions echoed through the autumn night.

Many of the male customers packed into Farren's were western businessmen, but there were fewer western women because many had been evacuated from the city. But neither the war nor the dearth of familiar partners had cramped Shanghai's nightlife; if anything, it was more frenetic. On the crowded dance floor Emily bumped into a young woman she knew as Jean, who came from South Africa. They had been introduced before but now Emily was puzzled because Jean 'looked at me ... as if she were not at all sure I would recognize her'.

The reason for Jean's uncertainty was that until recently she had been a star attraction in one of the city's high class brothels, and she was worried that she would be snubbed, or worse, called out and shamed. In fact Emily did not know Jean had been a prostitute, and when she did find out she didn't judge her for it, for she herself was on the wrong side of respectability and a sworn foe of hypocrisy and convention.

Emily also didn't know that Jean's real name was Lorraine

Murray and she came from Australia, not South Africa. The identity of Jean was part of an armour of lies that Lorraine wore to shield her from a censorious world, but it didn't protect her from her inner fears. She was haunted by the sense that she was an outcast, and not only because she had been a sex worker.

This would start becoming clear to Emily a few months later, when Lorraine moved into her home, beginning a lifelong friendship between the two women. Over the next decade Emily would guide Lorraine away from a life of banality, while for her part Lorraine would provide Emily with material for several books. In the first of these, the 1944 memoir *China to Me*, Lorraine appeared as Jean: beautiful, immature, foul-tempered and morally blind to the catastrophe engulfing China. Then in the 1947 novel *Miss Jill*, Lorraine appears in fictionalised guise as Jill, a younger woman struggling to take control of her life.

That night in Farren's, Lorraine was dancing with the Italian journalist Luigi Barzini, a rising star of Mussolini's Fascist regime. He was one of the flock of journalists who had arrived in Shanghai to cover the Sino-Japanese War, and he and Lorraine had just begun an affair which would be one of the great romances of her life. It was also Lorraine's introduction to the world of the foreign correspondent and in the coming years she would often be found in the company of journalists: not only Italian but American, British, Japanese and Australian as well. With Emily as her mentor, this new milieu would stimulate Lorraine's interest in politics and global affairs, books and writing – among the strands which, woven together, became her bridge to a new life.

In *China to Me* Emily tells how they had met the previous year, when a businessman nicknamed Dee Dee – 'a man in town, a wealthy broker' – had asked the writer a favour. Would she hold a party to introduce 'a young woman who was stranded in the city'? The young woman was Lorraine, and the party had not been a success. According to Emily, she 'was extraordinarily pretty and she looked just like the others in the way she dressed, but there was a something in her manner that made me look at her twice. She wasn't at all easy in her mind.' Next, Dee Dee invited Emily and Lorraine out to dinner at a Japanese restaurant. On this occasion, Emily discovered that Lorraine spoke fluent Japanese, which surprised her because Dee Dee had told her that she had just arrived from South Africa. And that was the last she saw of her until they met on the dance floor.

Then, a few months after that night at Farren's, Dee Dee called Emily again, to say that Lorraine had made a suicide attempt and to ask if she could come and see Emily to talk things over. The upshot was that Lorraine moved in, and was soon beginning to unburden herself to the writer. It turned out that Lorraine had spent two years working in Madam Louise's, a high class brothel, and that Dee Dee, having supported her to leave the sex industry, was now trying to get Lorraine to lead a more reputable life with the ultimate goal of her marrying a suitable man. And that, although in love with her, Dee Dee was unable to offer himself as a husband. Lorraine was, to use her own term, a 'demimondaine': one who lived on the boundary of prostitution, but Dee Dee's family belonged to Shanghai's elite and he could not expose them to the scandal that a marriage to Lorraine might entail were her former profession revealed.

In fact, Lorraine's suicide attempt had been triggered by a rebuff from Luigi Barzini, but their troubled affair was only one of her woes, her shame at having been a prostitute looming large among them. But why had she gone to work in a brothel in the first place? Emily's books tell the reader very little about

Lorraine's life before she arrived in China, only that she had previously been the mistress of a high Japanese official and that, when that relationship had ended, she had been passing through Shanghai and stayed on, eventually winding up in Madame Louise's.

But the real roots of her unhappiness stretched back to her earliest childhood.

One: Rainee
Adelaide 1910 – Sydney 1929

They fuck you up, your mum and dad.
They may not mean to, but they do.
They fill you with the faults they had
And add some extra, just for you.
Phillip Larkin

I

Shame

The thorns that I have reaped
Are of the tree I planted
They have cut me till I bleed
I should have known what fruit
Would come from such a tree.

Laura Murray

She grew up desperate to belong.

Over the course of her life Lorraine would appear in various guises—as the young mistress of an elder statesman, a sex worker, a counter-intelligence informant, a society matron and a late-blooming career woman—but she was first and foremost a daughter and a sister. To her family, she was Rainee—short for Lorraine—but being Rainee was never simple. As a child and then as a young woman, Lorraine's place in the family was ambiguous, and this in turn reflected her mother Laura's own insecurities.

During the 1910s, Laura gave birth to four children: Lorraine by one man, two boys and a girl by another. All four were born outside wedlock, and whilst the father of Lorraine's siblings would (eventually) be identified, her own father never was. If it had become known that Laura was an unmarried mother then she would have been branded as immoral and her children as illegitimate, and to ward off exposure she moved the family home, invented a dead husband and made up a false history of her life. While this succeeded in deflecting the censure of a moralising society, Laura lived in fear that she would be denounced, and this anxiety hung over her children like a cloud – even though they didn't know the reason for it.

Laura was born in 1890, in a tent on the banks of the flooded Darling River, and grew up in the far west region of New South Wales, a land of big skies and endless grey saltbush plains. Her father, William Treweek, was a labourer on a sheep station called *Moorara*, her mother Rachel died when she was six, and Laura grew into a considerable beauty. At the age of nineteen she was working as a domestic servant on *Cuthero* Station, on the right bank of the Darling, when she fell pregnant – according to family memory, the father was an itinerant worker. Laura travelled down to Adelaide and was taken in by the nuns at St Joseph's Refuge in the suburb of Fullarton, where she gave birth on 22 January 1910 to a baby girl named Laurinna Agnes Treweek – later, perhaps understandably, Laurinna preferred the name Lorraine. Laura left her daughter with foster parents in Adelaide and went back up the river.

During her life Lorraine would break many taboos and she broke her first one simply by existing, by being born illegitimate. This made her an outsider, and what followed made her doubly so, because the father of Laura's subsequent children refused to accept her as one of the family. He was the owner of *Cuthero*, the millionaire grazier and prince of the turf Ben Chaffey, and he was married into a pastoral dynasty whose interests were intertwined his own. In early 1913, Laura fell pregnant to Chaffey, and he decided to establish her as his mistress in Melbourne. But on her way to her new home, and apparently without Chaffey's blessing, Laura reclaimed the two-year old Lorraine from her foster family in Adelaide.

Over the next five years Chaffey regularly visited his secret second family, who were comfortably installed in a villa in suburban Melbourne. But he resented Lorraine's presence, and when he was in residence the little interloper was farmed out into the care of a Catholic nun. So as well as being removed from her foster parents, Lorraine experienced her birth mother's love only conditionally, when Chaffey wasn't around. Thus perched precariously on the edge of the nest, she watched it fill up with her siblings: first Peter, then John and then Margaret.

So Lorraine was the odd one out, and it's small wonder that Peter would say, years later, that she was riven with 'complexes' and 'insecurities' about their mother. In the 1980s, when Peter and Lorraine were living under the same roof, she would harp continually on her belief that Laura 'never loved' her. And it wasn't just her mother – Lorraine also keenly felt the absence of a father. But then, all of Laura's children suffered from the same lack, because Laura would soon cut Ben Chaffey out of all their lives.

Living in their Melbourne home, Laura somehow concealed from Peter, John and Margaret the fact that Chaffey was their father. To give all four of her children a nominal father, she had invented a husband named Chester Murray, who served overseas in the First World War and then conveniently died abroad during the Spanish influenza epidemic. Laura only began to open up about her relationship with Chaffey after his death in 1937, and then only to her eldest son Peter, and we don't know at what point Lorraine became explicitly aware that she was illegitimate.

Subconsciously, Lorraine must have known she was not the daughter of 'Chester Murray' – if only because she gave several different versions of the circumstances of her birth. In later life, she sometimes said that she had been born in Renmark, sometimes in Sydney, sometimes in Adelaide, and she would variously claim to be three, four and six years younger than she actually was. But this was only the beginning of her ambiguous relationship with truth: as time went on, following her mother's example, Lorraine enmeshed herself in a web of fiction.

She didn't just cover up her scarlet past, lie to get out of trouble and tell people what she thought they wanted to hear: she made stuff up for the fun of it. She became a spiritual sister of John Le Carré's beautiful and tragic demimondaine, the fabulist Lizzie Worthington, whose motto was 'new town, new leaf, new name'. Emily, who knew Lorraine better than anyone else, said that lying was her second nature; it was also her best defence against being found out, shamed and shunned.

'Cut me till I bleed'. The thorns in Laura's poem are a vivid expression of her self-lacerating sense of guilt, which made such an impression on her son Peter that sixty years later he could recite the words from memory.

Today it takes a real effort of imagination to understand how Laura felt. She was a product of the Victorian era, of a moral code that anathematized sex outside marriage, and although it was Chaffey who was the adulterer, as a woman it was Laura who would be the more condemned if their relationship was revealed. And her children would be illegitimate, a social condition which—according to the crusading Sydney clergyman the Reverend S.D. Yarrington—represented 'one of the darkest blots on the morality of the community'.

Yarrington was a self-appointed spokesman for the 'respectable' element of society and in the years when Laura's children were babies, he waged a well-publicised crusade against social evils like abortion and illegitimacy. As Yarrington insisted that the cure for these social ills was for women to avoid 'stepping over the narrow limits of the paths of virtue and morality', he was targeting single mothers like Laura—no wonder she felt so isolated and besieged. But it wasn't just unwed mothers who bore the brunt of these prejudices, it was their children too, because illegitimacy was regarded as almost a hereditary disease.

We get a sense of this from the autobiography of the art historian Bernard Smith who, like Lorraine, grew up illegitimate in Sydney in the 1920s. Smith's father disappeared—'shot through', in Australian parlance—and his mother couldn't afford to keep her infant son on her wages as a domestic servant. She was forced to take a job in rural Queensland, where the pay was better, and drifted away from him. Smith was fortunate to be taken in by a loving foster family; he was, as he put it, 'a lucky young bastard'. Even so, his boyhood was blighted by the sense that he was an outsider and when he came to write about his early life, it was his illegitimacy that defined it. Eventually united with his mother's family, he felt he was 'one of them and yet not one of them'; Lorraine must have felt somewhat the same way.

When Laura's children finally did find out that their parents had not been married, they were deeply affected by the revelation. All his life Peter reacted strongly to allusions to illegitimacy: as one of his daughters recalled, 'bastard was not a word used in our house'. In church, at school and in society generally, Laura and her children were bombarded by prejudice—including in the books they read.

Books were a constant presence in Lorraine's life. Not only was she an avid reader, she befriended writers, she typed their manuscripts, and in providing the inspiration for Emily's novel *Miss Jill* one could almost say Lorraine became a book herself. And she inherited this love of books, along with acute social anxiety, from Laura. A photo of the young Lorraine and her mother shows her sitting on a sofa reading, with Laura leaning over to explain something in the text, and fifty years later the two would reminisce about books that had been in the family home when she was growing up. But books reflect their times for both good and ill, and the works of the 19th century novelists – so beloved by Laura, Lorraine, Emily and their contemporaries – are full of warnings against the dangers of sexual transgressions. Charles Dickens' *David Copperfield* being a notable case in point.

Beset with prejudice and wracked with anxiety, in mid-1918 Laura abruptly broke off relations with Ben Chaffey and moved with her children to Sydney. Melbourne was Chaffey's town – and that of his wife and her Establishment family as well. Laura didn't want to stay there, maintaining the fiction of an absent husband and with the danger of being denounced as a jezebel lurking around every corner. She thought the subterfuge was having a bad effect on her children, and one which would grow worse as they grew older. Sydney offered the prospect of a clean slate: as a stranger there, there was less chance of her lies being exposed.

Chaffey respected Laura's decision to end their relationship, and continued to pay her an allowance – a very substantial one, amounting to five times the income of a working class family. And while money may not buy happiness, it can buy respectability, and so for a new family home Laura chose the affluent suburb of Warrawee on Sydney's upper North Shore. She and her children lived there in some style, keeping horses and employing several domestic servants – such as she would probably have remained had she not become Chaffey's mistress.

On arriving in Sydney, Laura had enrolled Lorraine at Kincoppal, a posh Catholic girls' boarding school in Elizabeth Bay, on the shores of Sydney Harbour. This was Lorraine's first glimpse of the Kings Cross and Potts Point area, which would become her favourite part of the city.

We don't know why Laura decided, in sending the eight-year-old Lorraine to a boarding school, to continue to exclude her from the family home. Chaffey was no longer around to object to her presence, but perhaps she felt she should maintain boundaries that he had previously insisted on. Or perhaps she had promised the nuns at St Joseph's that she would raise Lorraine as a Catholic – something else which, in an era of strong sectarian prejudice, marked Lorraine off from her siblings. Laura herself was an observant Anglican, and eventually Lorraine would herself be confirmed in the Anglican church. Nevertheless, she retained an attachment to Catholicism which would surface again at odd moments during her later life.

In any event, after some months Laura withdrew Lorraine from Kincoppal because she was 'too delicate' – which sounds like she was deeply unhappy. Her next school that we know of was the bluestocking academy Abbotsleigh Girls School, within walking distance of their home in Warrawee. Lorraine and her little sister Margaret were enrolled there in February 1923 and later that year their brother Peter entered the elite King's School, where wealthy pastoralists sent their sons; two years later their other brother John followed him there. But by now the teenage Lorraine's relationship with her mother was growing stormy. Years later, John commented that Laura 'found Lorraine quite difficult ... I think Mother was frightened that she would undermine the rest of us children'. Margaret had similar memories, recalling that Lorraine had been 'very rebellious (*and*) wouldn't conform with the modes of society'.

This may be why, just after her fifteenth birthday, Lorraine was sent as a boarder to the New England Girls School (NEGS), in Armidale in the Northern Tablelands region of New South

Wales. Here she gained her Intermediate Certificate, showing she had completed three years of secondary schooling, but when she left NEGS she took no fond memories with her.

The students were mostly the daughters of New England's wealthy pastoralists and this made Lorraine, again, an outsider. The poet Judith Wright, who attended the school around the same time, recalled how those girls like Lorraine who came from city homes were assumed to be guilty of shameful behaviour—why else would they be exiled to the bush?—and shunned by the other students. Small wonder that Lorraine recalled that 'I always was unhappy at school'.

We have one sad snapshot of this unhappy schoolgirl. At King's School, her brother Peter had befriended a boy belonging to the Dangar family, leading members of New England's pastoral aristocracy. One holiday Peter was invited to stay at the Dangar's grand home, *Palmerston*, just outside Armidale, and when he was there Lorraine was invited out from NEGS. As Peter recalled, 'we would be sitting up in this beautiful big dining room, with housemaids all dressed up ... Lorraine was a big fat girl around sixteen, very plump and had a big moony looking face ... Mrs Dangar was a snobbish sort of person (*and*) would be patronising towards Lorraine ... (*she*) used to say nasty things to her'.

If this was the sort of bullying Lorraine faced as a guest, we can imagine what she had to endure at school itself. And perhaps this was one reason why, when her transformation from ugly duckling to exquisite swan was complete, she took such pleasure in snobbery herself.

Out of school and back in Sydney, in mid-1927 Lorraine enrolled in Stott & Underwood's Business College on Pitt Street, beginning her long march to competency in the skills of a stenographer typist. This was an occupation which would figure largely in her life.

Nowadays stenography is just another of the myriad jobs abolished by the information revolution, but for much of the last century it was a major form of skilled employment for women. It was seen as a liberating, respectable occupation, particularly for middle class women who regarded working as a domestic servant or in a factory as beneath them, and Lorraine – though hating the grind – persevered with stenography courses on and off for the next fifteen years. Eventually typing would become her mainstay: she would take pride in her skill and saw it as opening the way to economic independence and social acceptance. Foreshadowing another of her adult skills, she also took night classes at the Berlitz School of Languages on George Street. And then she got a job with the *Sun*, an afternoon tabloid newspaper.

In the 1920s Australian newspapers had begun to expand their coverage of 'women's issues', and Lorraine worked in the *Sun's* 'Topics for Women' section. A typical section – to take that published on her 20th birthday – led with an article about Australia's maternal mortality rate. Then came social news, and a report from London about how the current craze for ice-skating was leading to a decline in attendance at dinner dances. The bulk of the page was taken out with advertisements for clothes, cosmetics and medicines.

Did Lorraine ever consider journalism as a career? It would have been a difficult ambition to pursue, but not impossible. At the time she was working for the *Sun*, there were scores of female journalists employed by Australian mastheads, among them the *Sun* contributors Ernestine Hill, later a noted book author, and Dorothy Jenner, who filed her column 'Andrea' from Europe and the United States. But if Lorraine did have ambitions to become a journalist, these would have been crushed by the onset of the Great Depression.

We have only glimpses of Lorraine in her late teens. One night at the family home in Warrawee when their mother had gone out, Lorraine invited her friends around for a party which got out of hand. From the upstairs landing, her siblings watched with fascination as she and her friends did what drunken teenagers do when there are no adults around. Then there is a newspaper report of a Miss Lorraine Murray making her society debut in July 1928 at a charity ball. We don't know for certain if this was our Rainee, but she was in the right place at the right time. Another mentions a Lorraine Murray being fined and shamed for travelling on the train without a ticket, which again equally well could be her. And at some point she moved out of the family home in Warrawee to a flat in Darling Point, just across the water from her old school Kincoppal.

From a financial point of view, Lorraine was a fortunate young woman. The trauma she must have felt at being fostered out, then excluded from the family home, and then sent to boarding school, would have been very real. But Laura's success at passing for a widow, together with the substantial allowance she received from Chaffey, had shielded her children from the consequences of her violation of a hypocritical moral code. Laura feared being judged as an unwed mother, but Bernard Smith's mother had to give up her son because she couldn't afford to keep him. Lorraine may have been bullied at school for being an outsider, but Smith was beaten up by his classmates for being a bastard.

Laura's children had the best schooling available—quite a few of Lorraine's peers from Abbotsleigh and NEGS went on to university. And when Lorraine moved out of the Warrawee home to live independently in a flat in Darling Point, Laura paid her rent—with Chaffey's money. As she neared the age of twenty, Lorraine's life was one of upper-middle class privilege.

But that was just about to evaporate.

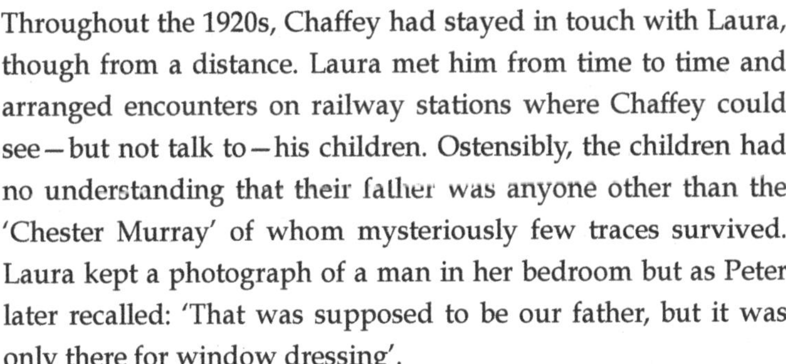

Throughout the 1920s, Chaffey had stayed in touch with Laura, though from a distance. Laura met him from time to time and arranged encounters on railway stations where Chaffey could see—but not talk to—his children. Ostensibly, the children had no understanding that their father was anyone other than the 'Chester Murray' of whom mysteriously few traces survived. Laura kept a photograph of a man in her bedroom but as Peter later recalled: 'That was supposed to be our father, but it was only there for window dressing'.

By now Chaffey was acclaimed as 'one of the continent's greatest pastoralists'. There are thousands of newspaper reports of his doings, mostly in connection with his racing activities—he was nicknamed 'lucky Ben Chaffey' because of his success on the racecourse and also because his pastoral empire seemed immune to setbacks like drought. He was a director of woolbrokers Goldsbrough, Mort and Co. and Chairman of the Board of United Distillers. He and his wife were regular fixtures in the society pages of the Melbourne newspapers. Chaffey's apotheosis came when he was made Chairman of the Victorian Amateur Turf Club—now folded into the Melbourne Racing Club. This was not a man who would have welcomed exposure as the father of an illegitimate family.

But then Chaffey's luck ran out. The effect of a three-year drought in the far west, combined with the Wall Street Crash of October 1929, wrecked his finances. He had to retrench, and he could no longer afford to maintain his secret family at anything like the same level as before. So Laura and her children suffered the same sort of reduction in circumstances as did unfortunate genteel families in 19th century novels, like Jane Austen's Dashwoods – a comparison they would have recognised.

It must have been a terrible shock. Lorraine's brothers had to leave school; Chaffey took them on as jackeroos and they embarked on the rigorous apprenticeship of a stockman. Margaret, only eleven, was kept on at school. Laura herself went from luxury to bare subsistence; her allowance was cut by nine-tenths and she went to live on a farm outside Nowra, on the South Coast of New South Wales.

But Lorraine managed to dodge the whole catastrophe.

II

The Diplomat and the Courtesan

Mr. Tokugawa has left his wife and children in Japan, probably to give himself time to make necessary and adequate preparations for their reception.

Sydney *Sunday Times*

Lorraine's transformation from a restive young Sydney woman to the star of a high class Shanghai brothel began one night in early 1928.

She was going around the tables in a nightclub in her capacity as a junior reporter for the *Sun*. The social rounds, as they were known, involved asking patrons their names so that they could be printed in social columns of the paper. This was how Lorraine came to meet the man Emily Hahn described in her novel *Miss Jill* as 'Botchan' and in her memoir *China to Me* as Lorraine's 'Prince'. His name was Tokugawa Iemasa and at the time Lorraine met him he was Tokyo's most senior diplomat in Australasia, with the title of Consul General to Australia and New Zealand. She was eighteen and he was forty-three.

For the reporter, one of the pitfalls of the social rounds was that there was a risk that one or either of the couple they approached might be married to someone else. In fact Sydney was so straightlaced the chances of anyone publicly flaunting their adultery was slight. But on that night, however, Tokugawa probably *was* accompanied by his mistress, the Swedish artist Ella Strom, a remarkable woman described by historian Elinor Wrobel as a bohemian 'courtesan'.

Over the coming year, Lorraine and Tokugawa would become acquainted; just how well acquainted is not clear. Tokugawa had his daughter Toyoko living with him in the Consul's residence, and some years later he would employ Lorraine as Toyoko's companion – so it seems the two girls had spent considerable time together in Sydney. Lorraine's mother Laura also met Tokugawa and Ella Strom, and to the Murray women the Tokugawa ménage must have seemed like visitors from another planet, a glamorous world of diplomatic receptions, ocean liners and unhallowed liaisons. But this little circle of acquaintance soon disbanded: Ella left Sydney in July 1928 and the following year Tokugawa was transferred to the Canadian capital of Ottawa.

Then in 1931, Lorraine travelled to Ottawa and became Tokugawa's mistress. Their relationship lasted two years, and it determined the whole course of her life.

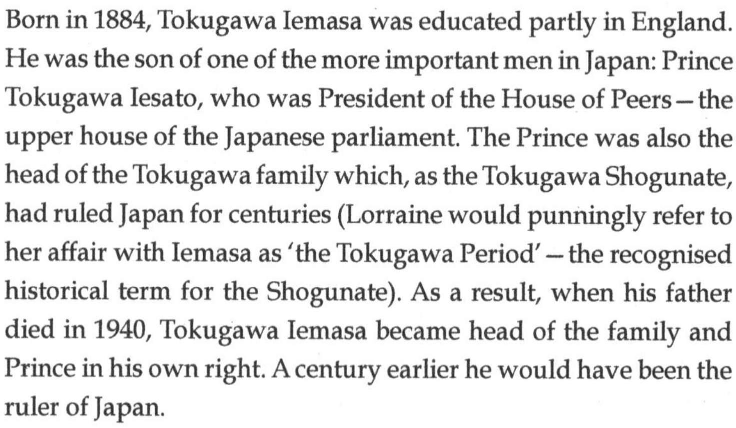

Born in 1884, Tokugawa Iemasa was educated partly in England. He was the son of one of the more important men in Japan: Prince Tokugawa Iesato, who was President of the House of Peers – the upper house of the Japanese parliament. The Prince was also the head of the Tokugawa family which, as the Tokugawa Shogunate, had ruled Japan for centuries (Lorraine would punningly refer to her affair with Iemasa as 'the Tokugawa Period' – the recognised historical term for the Shogunate). As a result, when his father died in 1940, Tokugawa Iemasa became head of the family and Prince in his own right. A century earlier he would have been the ruler of Japan.

Tokugawa's career flourished in the period known as the Taisho Democracy, which lasted from 1905 to 1926. He had diplomatic postings in London and Beijing, and a stint as private secretary to Foreign Minister Kato Takaaki, who subsequently served a term as Prime Minister, during which he bolstered Japan's nascent democracy by (very cautiously) extending the franchise. The Taisho era was a relatively liberal interval of reform and openness to Western ideas, an openness embodied by Tokugawa—particularly in his enjoyment of the pleasures the West had to offer.

Behind this impressive façade, Tokugawa's domestic situation was messy. His wife, with whom he had four children, had accompanied him on his second posting to London, but had returned to Tokyo in 1922. That was the year Ella Strom became Tokugawa's mistress, and their story bears telling for two reasons. It was a preview of his affair with Lorraine because in both cases, Tokugawa's liaison with a Western woman irritated the Japanese ruling elite of which he was supposed to be an exemplary member—Japan, after all, had its own code of respectability. The other reason was that his affairs with Ella and with Lorraine overlapped.

In many ways Ella's history mirrored that of Lorraine's mother Laura. Born in rural Sweden in 1889, Ella had escaped her provincial home at a young age. In London she found a patron, the wealthy Conservative politician Frederick Leverton Harris, who was married and twenty-five years her senior, and in 1909 she gave birth to his daughter, whom she passed off as a niece to disguise her illegitimacy. Ella's relationship with Harris lasted more than a decade, during which he supported her career as a poet and artist.

Then, ditching the politician, Ella began her liaison with Tokugawa. But in 1924 the niece of Tokugawa's wife married the

Japanese Crown Prince, soon to become the Emperor Hirohito; as a result Tokugawa's affair with Ella now impinged directly on the Chrysanthemum Throne. Following (false) rumours that Ella had had a child by him, Tokugawa was recalled to Tokyo. From there he was posted to Sydney, arriving in December 1925 together with Toyoko, then aged eleven. His wife and his other children remained in Tokyo.

If the authorities had calculated that the privations of life in remote Australia would deter Ella from joining him there, they were wrong. Ella's first stay in Sydney lasted seven months, and while she did indeed despise most things Australian, she enjoyed Tokugawa's official residence, which had sweeping harbour views and access to a tiny secluded beach. Then in November 1926, she embarked for Canada on her way to England, and among her fellow passengers was the musician and composer Percy Grainger.

Still ranked among the 20th century's notable composers, in his day the Melbourne-born Grainger was a global celebrity. A sado-masochist obsessed with the memory of his mother, among his more enduring eccentricities is his bequest to the University of Melbourne of a substantial museum—dedicated to himself. A vanity project if ever there was one, the Grainger Museum preserves the correspondence between Ella and Tokugawa, the window through which we can observe Tokugawa's affair with Lorraine.

Fatefully, Ella resembled Grainger's mother, and the composer flung himself at her feet. He escorted her as far as New York and at their parting he presented her with $5,000, about four year's wages for an American factory worker. The following year he pursued her to England and in September she accepted his proposal of marriage—but it took her a while to break the news to Tokugawa. In December 1927, Ella arrived back in Sydney; this time she stayed for eight months, and it was during this period that she met Lorraine and her mother. There would have been some interesting undercurrents to the meeting between Ella and Laura; the two women had similar histories but very different temperaments. Ella was cosmopolitan, risk-taking, and polyamorous; Laura was a church-going 'widow', obsessed with bourgeois respectability. One wonders how much of their hidden lives the two revealed to each other.

Leaving Sydney again, Ella travelled back to America and in August 1928 she and Grainger were married in front of a concert audience in Los Angeles' Hollywood Bowl. His wedding gift to her was the bridal song *To a Nordic Princess*, which was performed at the ceremony by an enormous orchestra. Her wedding gift to him was a kangaroo hide riding crop. Given this playful hint of the connubial bliss to come, one might have thought that Ella had given up Tokugawa—but nothing was further from her mind. She regarded 'Masa' (as she called him) as bound to her by unbreakable ties, and Grainger no more than a tedious complication—a mere financial necessity. At least, this is the way she put it in her letters to Tokugawa, in which she was often running her new husband down—'talks incessantly ... quite rough, almost like a peasant'.

On taking up his new posting in Ottawa, Tokugawa regularly visited the Graingers in their home in White Plains New York, and they visited him in Canada. Ella had laid Tokugawa under epistolary siege: they often exchanged letters twice a week, and her letters imply that their intimacy continued—or at least that she wished it were so. She emphasized that she viewed her marriage to Grainger as an open one: she was, she told 'Masa', 'free to come and go as I please'.

Whether she kept up a sexual relationship with Tokugawa or not, she never surrendered her emotional claims on him and the tone of her letters is one of perpetual jealous complaint. She constantly berates him, he apologises over and over again: 'I am sorry', 'I am sorry'. When on one occasion in 1931 their correspondence briefly flagged, she belaboured him with accusations of infidelity. He replied wearily: 'No, it was not due to no romance or any similar "affair" that I did not write. Such a thing is completely out of my mind these days—except that I always look back to the old days and console myself for the fact that my life history is adorned with the happiest recollection of beautiful things'.

But just as Tokugawa was assuring Ella that romance was now all in his past, he was coaching Lorraine on how to get past Canadian immigration officials.

Emily Hahn would later describe Lorraine at this time as a 'dreamy discontented girl', and this discontented girl was now in the grip of that quintessentially Australian desire—to get out of Australia.

Despite the onset of the Depression she had managed to stay in her Darling Point flat. We don't know if she had kept her job at the *Sun*, but given the economic climate there was a real danger she would be forced to join Laura out in the sticks (an Australian term for 'the boondocks') behind Nowra, a life of chickens, firewood and cowshit. It must have seemed to Lorraine that just as she had begun to contemplate some of the good things life can offer, fate had snatched them away, and she was determined not to submit to that verdict. It took her two years to get away, but she succeeded.

She faced a lot of obstacles. To leave the country she needed a passport, a return ticket, sufficient funds to support herself abroad and, to gain entry to places like the United States and

Canada she had to have invitations from suitable residents in those countries. *Suitable* residents, because above all Lorraine had to overcome widespread concern about the trafficking of young women, then known as 'white slavery'. There were some grounds for this concern: there was a history of young Australian women being trafficked to brothels abroad, including to Shanghai. Asians were regarded as particularly predatory, with sex-crazed Chinese featuring prominently among the Reverend Yarrington's obsessions. As a result, young women applying to travel abroad were closely screened by the authorities, and their families informed of their plans.

Fears of 'white slavery' were amplified in popular culture. In 1930 Sydney cinemas were showing *Shanghai Lady*, a Hollywood production tagged as 'The story of every white girl adrift in the Orient!' Replete with stereotypical portraits of Chinese as pimps and murderers, it starred Mary Nolan as a young American in Shanghai who tries to put her time as a prostitute behind her.

Within a few years, Lorraine would be living the plot.

The stages in Lorraine's protracted escape from Australia were recorded by the passport authorities, whose offices were in the old Customs House on Sydney's Circular Quay. This was where, in October 1929, she presented herself to apply for a passport, saying that she intended to travel to Hawaii chaperoned by family friends, a couple called the McDonalds – who, however, were not available to confirm her claim. She also said that she wanted to leave the very next day. The officials told her to come back with her mother: she never did.

This failed pier-head jump came at the very moment that Tokugawa was crossing the Pacific to take up his new appointment as the Japanese Minister (ambassador) to Ottawa, so she may have been trying to join him. And this raises the possibility that either or both were infatuated with the other—and that they may already have become intimate. We don't know, but when a year later Lorraine wrote to Tokugawa, angling for an invitation to join him in Ottawa, his reply was cautious. He said that she would be welcome to visit as a tourist, but that because of mass unemployment in Canada it would be difficult for her to enter the country if she was intending to get a job there.

The next step in Lorraine's escape came in March 1931, when she again visited the Customs House. Things didn't go smoothly this time either; when the officials asked Lorraine if she had her mother's permission to travel she said she did, but then lied about Laura's whereabouts. Some days later the plot thickened when Mr McDonald—with whom Lorraine had previously proposed travelling to Hawaii—called at Customs House to state his belief that she was in moral danger and should not be given a passport at all. McDonald said he and his wife, who were 'well acquainted' with Lorraine, had come to know that she had a ticket to North America which had been paid for by a suspicious unknown man.

This unknown man was Tokugawa. In the previous six months his attitude to Lorraine had warmed considerably: he was now eager for her to join him in Ottawa and was coaching her on how to get past the immigration authorities on her arrival in Canada. He explained how, to dispel their suspicions, she should tell them that she would be staying at Ottawa's most expensive hotel, the Chateau Laurier. She should tell officials 'that your mother's friend in Ottawa will look after you, and again if absolutely necessary you may mention my name or rather "the Japanese Minister" as that friend. I shall also treat you "officially" as "a daughter of someone I know" rather than as "a friend of mine"'. It was all very strange. Ostensibly Lorraine was just the daughter of someone Tokugawa had met briefly a few years ago, yet now he was coaching her on how to get around Canadian border controls so that she could move in with him. Clearly, she had got under his skin.

And when Lorraine next appeared at the passport office, she had all her ducks in a row. She had a written invitation from Tokugawa. She said that she was receiving an allowance of £20 per month, that she had her mother's permission to travel abroad and that her mother would confirm all this to the authorities. One wonders how Lorraine managed to win over Laura who was, after all, no stranger to moral danger herself. But she did, because Laura rang the Customs House from Nowra to state that Lorraine's plan to visit Canada had 'her full knowledge and consent'. She backed up everything her daughter had said—including her claim she was receiving a monthly allowance of £20.

Laura also said that she herself was a friend of Tokugawa's and that she was prepared to financially support Lorraine in Canada if required. And in addition to all these reassurances, she outlined a back-up plan; if the arrangements for Lorraine to stay with Tokugawa somehow fell through, then Laura knew a respectable married woman in America who would take her in charge. This was 'Mrs Grainger', Tokugawa's former—and perhaps still current—mistress Ella Strom.

It was a notable triumph for Lorraine. She had fended off the interfering McDonalds, won over her mother and bamboozled the bureaucracy. She was escaping from Australia and, although it was two years since they had last met, Tokugawa was paying for it all. Not for the last time, we are struck by her powers of persuasion. Soon she would be ensconced in the ambassadorial residence in Ottawa, nominally as Toyoko's 'companion', but in fact as Tokugawa's mistress.

Two: Jean
Ottawa 1931 – Shanghai 1939

... one of the most beautiful women I have ever seen
Emily Hahn *China to Me*

I

'The Tokugawa Period'

This is no sob story of betrayed maidenhood ...
Emily Hahn, *China to Me*

Emily Hahn's books are not the only evidence for Lorraine's affair with Tokugawa Iemasa. When questioned by an Australian intelligence official in 1940, Lorraine 'made no bones' about the nature of their relationship. But most eloquent is the fact that in the depths of the worst economic depression the world had ever known Lorraine lived a life of luxury, travelling around the world and staying in luxury hotels, a lifestyle out of all proportion to her nominal domestic position.

Toyoko arrived in Canada from Japan in July 1931. Taking a break from his diplomatic duties, her father met her in Vancouver and they travelled slowly back to Ottawa, taking in the tourist sights on the way. Lorraine arrived around the same time and accompanied the Tokugawas on this trip, sending Laura postcards of the Rocky Mountains scenery. After this, there is a break of nine months in the record, during which her affair with Tokugawa started. Or, perhaps, resumed.

Lorraine herself left no record of her time with Tokugawa, but in *China to Me* Emily gives an account of what Lorraine told her. The essence of this was that their relationship

> *was staggeringly romantic ... she was eager and happy to join the prince's household. She liked him. This is no sob story of betrayed maidenhood ... Her life was merry and luxurious ... she learned how to behave at diplomatic receptions, and how to dress, and how to keep her mouth shut ...*

Taken literally, the comment about 'maidenhood' suggests that Lorraine had had some sexual experience prior to joining Tokugawa in Canada. If they had been intimate while he was in Sydney, this might help explain why he went to such lengths to arrange for her to join him in Canada—because he wanted to renew their affair. But she was twenty-one when she left Australia, and may well have had other partners.

Miss Jill tells a similar story to *China to Me*: that Lorraine had a wonderful time as Tokugawa's mistress.

> *Hers was no shockingly brutal seduction ...* (he) *was rich, and that thrilled her; he was different, and that pleased her more than his wealth ... And he was kind in his way, which could almost be called a fatherly way ...'*

The choice of the word 'fatherly' was an acute one: many years later Lorraine would say to Emily that she had spent her 'younger days in search of a Father', to compensate for the one she never knew. She found one in Tokugawa, and she learnt a lot from him. As Emily put it, Lorraine 'spent the first years of her career not as a European whore but as a Japanese mistress. There is a good deal of difference between the two'.

In his letters to Ella, Tokugawa's references to Lorraine are paternal, amused, sometimes irritated—as if the Australian was a mere child, to be indulged, but not taken too seriously. This was a show of detachment to hide the fact that she was his new mistress, but the subterfuge didn't work for long. And when Ella found out that Lorraine had succeeded her, she was not happy.

In 1932, the Tokugawa and Grainger households were often in each other's company. In April Percy Grainger was guest conductor at a concert in Toronto. Writing to Ella, Tokugawa said that Lorraine would be one of his party attending this concert, and commented on how much she had 'grown' since they had first met her in Sydney, four years before. Another letter told how the concert had been followed by a society dinner, at which the son of the host sat between Lorraine and Toyoko. Tokugawa reported 'The boy seemed to have been charmed so much by Lorraine that he handed her a little slip of paper as we were leaving, & there's no doubt it was a little piece of flirting.'

The following month Tokugawa made plans to travel with Toyoko and Lorraine to White Plains for the Westchester County Music Festival, an event patronised by the New York elite and one in which Percy Grainger would feature prominently. But by now Ella's suspicions of Lorraine were fully aroused, and she refused to invite the young Australian into the Grainger home, forcing Tokugawa to mediate between the two women. Caught in the crossfire, he sounds grumpy, protesting that he didn't want 'to be bothered much about this young lady': but once more Lorraine's powers of persuasion prevailed and she was received at White Plains. On his return to Ottawa, Tokugawa – still trying to divert Ella's suspicions from his new relationship – told her how Lorraine had now fallen for a young Japanese man. Which may well have been true: Lorraine was no longer an ungainly teenager but a beautiful woman, and the men swarming around his radiant young mistress cost Tokugawa agonies of jealousy.

This story of high society rivalry between old and new lovers could have been written by Noel Coward—whose comedy *Private Lives*, written in Shanghai, had just closed on Broadway. But while Coward's sparkling comedies represent the lighter side of the Thirties, there were dark clouds gathering on the horizon.

In September 1931, just as Lorraine had been settling into Tokugawa's residence in Ottawa, the Japanese Army staged a fake terrorist attack in Manchuria and then 'responded' to it by launching a full scale invasion of the Chinese province. This was the so-called 'Mukden Incident', and Tokugawa published opinion pieces in the Canadian press defending the Japanese invasion as simply an 'anti-bandit' campaign, necessary to maintain law and order. Then, eight months later, ultra-nationalists mounted a coup d'état in Tokyo: the coup failed but the Prime Minister was assassinated in the attempt. Tokugawa's father, Prince Tokugawa Iesato, was also targeted by the plotters, but the assassin sent to kill him lost his nerve. It was another sign that modernisers like Prince Tokugawa and his son, well disposed to the West, were losing control to the militarists who would lead Japan to war and disaster.

Meanwhile, the rivalry between old and new lovers persisted. Lorraine started intercepting Ella's letters to Tokugawa and he, trying to defuse the situation, suggested to Ella that she write to his office address rather than to his home. But she took this to mean that she was being downgraded in deference to Lorraine, and flew into a rage. As always, Tokugawa abased himself before her: 'I didn't for a moment place anybody else's feelings before yours'.

Given this tension, it must have come as something of a relief to Tokugawa when in October 1932 he put Lorraine on a ship for England. He wasn't casting her off—far from it—but he would have been happy to let things cool down a bit. Always conscious that their relationship might embarrass the Imperial Palace, there was now an added consideration: Toyoko, a first cousin of the Empress, was approaching the age of marriage. A husband of suitable rank had to be found for her, and it would not look well if it were revealed that her beautiful *gaijin* 'companion' had in fact been her father's mistress.

In December, Toyoko was presented at a Debutante Ball at the Ottawa Country Club, which the Graingers attended. But even with Lorraine on the far side of the Atlantic, Ella's jealousy was still raw. Early in the new year she confronted Tokugawa about his relationship with Lorraine; in his reply, he denied that the younger woman had 'conquered his heart' and continued on: 'I don't know what she is really doing in England. The latest news was that she was intending to go to Algiers or somewhere ...'.

But Tokugawa was dissembling, because just days before he had written these words, Lorraine had embarked for Japan. To do this she needed money for her fare, a visa, and contacts in Japan, and only he could have helped her with these. In fact he had decided to establish her in Tokyo, where he himself was due to return. And when they were reunited in Japan in April 1933, they embarked on the last chapter of their relationship.

According to *China to Me*, Lorraine was at first lodged in Tokugawa's family home. But his wife objected to her presence, so the Australian was boarded out to a geisha house where, between visits from Tokugawa, Lorraine acquired a smattering of the arts of the geisha. During her eight months in Tokyo, Lorraine's competence in spoken Japanese rose to a level where she could converse in Japanese homes and shops, as well as deal with officials.

And now, just as the authorities had previously recalled Tokugawa from London because of his affair with Ella, they decided to quash his scandalous liaison with his new foreign mistress. Lorraine was arrested and deported, with Tokugawa left powerless to object. Farewelling her with a large gift of money, he enjoined her to go home to Australia and live a virtuous life with her family. The police escorted her to Nagasaki and put her on a ship bound for Shanghai, from where she could get a connecting passage home to Australia.

II

Johnny Jean of Connaught Road

It took more than one man to change my name to Shanghai Lily

Marlene Dietrich, *Shanghai Express*

LORRAINE DISEMBARKED in Shanghai on 25th September 1933. What began as a stopover turned into a stay lasting nearly six years.

Over the previous century the city had emerged as China's main entrepôt, and the most spectacular beneficiaries of this growth were its foreign colonial elite. They lived mainly in an enclave—itself made up of two districts, the International Settlement and the French Concession—in the heart of the city.

When Lorraine arrived, the population of this foreign enclave was well over a million, but it was lorded over by just twenty thousand 'Europeans'—a term which Emily, with her disdain for cant, would dismiss as a 'clumsy circumlocution for white'. Another term for them was 'Shanghailanders', which the historian Robert Bickers has characterised as 'an identity available to all who subscribed to a parochial political vision'—that is to say, a vision of racial superiority and their own importance. Shanghailander may be a clumsy portmanteau but it is a useful term, because it kept its currency well after the people to whom it referred had left China. Lorraine thought of herself as one for the rest of her life.

Though united by race, these 'Europeans' were divided by class: the social gap between, say, the English company executive and the Scottish police constable was if anything greater in colonial Shanghai than it was in London. Then there were the Russian refugees who had fled the Bolshevik revolution, who were treated as a race apart. Estimates of their numbers are even more elastic than are those for the other European population, but according to one count there were some twenty-five thousand Russians in Shanghai in the early 1930s—and their numbers increased rapidly later in the decade. Then there were the non-European foreigners in the foreign enclave, including the Sikh and Vietnamese policemen recruited from British India and French Indochina. But by far the most numerous foreigners were the Japanese, who had their own quarter—Hongkou—in the north eastern portion of the International Settlement.

And all these foreigners were just a tiny island in a Chinese sea, manifest in the fact that the foreign enclave was surrounded by the Chinese districts known as the Greater Shanghai Municipality. Despite this, the foreign enclave was outside Chinese jurisdiction and many regarded it as a bastion of racism and injustice and its existence as an affront to national dignity. The writer Wu Zhouliu, for example, saw the foreign enclave as a 'centre of big power extortion', and the 'arrogance and disdain' displayed towards the Chinese by the foreigners—including the Japanese—moved him to fury.

And yet by the time Lorraine arrived in the city, the privileged existence of the foreign enclave had only a few years to run. The Republic of China, under the Kuomintang Party of Premier Chiang Kai-shek, had recovered somewhat from the anarchy of the Warlord Era. True, the Republic faced the dire threat of Japanese aggression which would soon all but overwhelm it, but taken together, Chinese revival and Japanese militarism spelt the end for the European colonial ascendancy in China. And another force, even more potent, was stirring: the Chinese Communist Party. Though suppressed in both the foreign enclave and the Chinese suburbs, the CCP maintained an underground presence in the city.

Shanghai was the cockpit of geopolitical rivalry between the various powers vying for influence in China, and it was seething with spies. They were so common that the Australian journalist Peter Russo—a frequent visitor to the city—would recall that 'one of the most enthralling pastimes for interested bystanders at the Cathay Hotel was to try to guess who was spying for which Certain Power'. And as it happens the best source for Lorraine's first few months in Shanghai is a file compiled by the Shanghai Municipal Police (SMP) at the behest of the British Secret Intelligence Service, MI6. This opens with a request to investigate Lorraine, who

> *... according to her own story was employed for two years, prior to 1933, by the Japanese Minister to Canada in the capacity of nurse or governess to his children: was brought back by him to Japan which she left six months ago to come to Shanghai ... I would particularly request that the enquiries should be conducted in such a way as to cause her no alarm. It will also be most interesting if you could discover whether or not she is in personal contact now with any Japanese ...*

The 'I' of the memo was Harold Steptoe, the senior representative of the MI6 in China. He may have suspected Lorraine of spying for the Japanese or, given her access to Tokugawa, he may even have been considering her as a potential recruit to spy on the Japanese. As it turned out Lorraine did not go to work for Steptoe, but this is the first record of her presence on the periphery of the intelligence world, where she would hover for the next two decades.

Several sources tell us that on her arrival in Shanghai, Lorraine fell in love with an Italian, and the SMP file identifies him as one Lionello Sanseverino. Starting in December 1933, he and Lorraine were staying in separate rooms in the upscale Weida Hotel on the Avenue Joffre, now Huaihai Road, in the French Concession. On the basis that he was paying her hotel bill, the SMP file recorded that Lorraine was being 'kept' by Sanseverino; it also noted that Sanseverino's family was 'very wealthy and highly respectable'. Indeed, the Italian ambassador himself actually called on the young man at the hotel—which sounds like his influential family had asked the Foreign Ministry in Rome to keep an eye on him.

Lorraine had checked into the Weida under the surname Lee. We don't know why; perhaps she was worried that the Japanese authorities might be checking to see whether she had actually returned to Australia. The SMP investigator followed up a tip that she was working as a 'taxi dancer'—one who danced with customers in a nightclub for a fee. This was an occupation regarded as a step towards, or a cover for, outright prostitution. But the SMP found that rather than hanging out in seedy nightclubs, Lorraine was in fact keeping regular office hours and moreover, that in the hotel register she had stated her occupation as 'stenographer'. This suggest that, not for the last time, Lorraine had gone back to business school to improve her stenography.

So how did Lorraine become a prostitute? She herself never said, and the only source that sheds any light on her recruitment into the sex industry is the novel *Miss Jill,* whose title character is loosely based on Lorraine. But Jill is portrayed as a stereotypical victim of 'white slavery' and an ingénue—which Lorraine was not. Jill was trafficked, but it's not clear that this was Lorraine's own experience.

In the novel Jill, on her way from Nagasaki, is offered a job working as a nanny for an American family in Shanghai. Attracted by the idea she stops over, but the job offer falls through and she gets stranded. Swept along by the glamour of Shanghai, Jill falls in love with a dodgy Hungarian count, who promises marriage then steals her money. He turns out to be a pimp, and after managing her himself for a while he turns her over to the proprietor of a high class brothel in the International Settlement.

There's no reason to assume Lorraine's role was as passive as Jill's. The teenage Jill falls prey to the pimp because she is naïve, whereas Lorraine, now rising twenty-four, was more experienced—a point Emily emphasises in *China to Me*. She had more agency. By the time she arrived in Shanghai, she had been travelling abroad and living in foreign cities, sometimes on her own, for several years. And, lavishly supported by Tokugawa, she had developed a taste for the good life.

So Lorraine may well have chosen to work in the sex industry—though if she did, it was in a time and a place that didn't offer her many other options. Because of the Great Depression, employment opportunities for Europeans in Shanghai had dried up, and any respectable work she could do, someone else—Chinese, or Russian refugee—would do for less. But in that case, why didn't she just go back to Australia? Even if she had lost all her money, like Jill, she could have contacted her family for help, or applied to the consular authorities for a passage home. But this would have meant exchanging her dreams of a glamorous life abroad for the reality of rural drudgery in Australia, sharing a cottage with her mother. And the flies.

And there was another underlying reason Lorraine became a sex worker: opportunity was rife. Gender relations in Shanghai—both European and Chinese—were mediated by commercial sex to a degree that outside observers found astonishing. Graham Greene's comment about Havana in the 1950s—'One sold sex or one bought it—immaterial which, but it was never given away'—might well also have applied to Shanghai between the wars. Not for nothing was the city's nicknamed 'The Whore of the Orient'.

The sex industry in which Lorraine went to work blended the traditions of a Chinese city with the prejudices of the colonial enclave in its midst.

The established European brothel district was known as 'The Line', situated at the northern end of Kiangse (now Jiangxi) Road, which ran parallel to the riverside Bund in the International Settlement. In the 1910s and 1920s one of its most famous houses was run by Gracie Gale, who embodied the connection between the sex industries of Shanghai and the West Coast of America. The Australian journalist Percy Finch, who devoted twelve pages of his memoir of life in Shanghai to Gale and her milieu, commented that she had 'pushed the American girl to the top of her profession. What Ming was to porcelain and the Rolls Royce was to cars, the American girl was to commercial vice in Shanghai'.

Following the prejudices of the times, Gale's establishment was closed to Chinese—whether as prostitutes or patrons. But this exclusion of Chinese from Shanghai's European brothels broke down after the Russian Revolution, when waves of destitute Russian refugee women arrived in the city and began to accept Chinese men as customers. In the face of this competition from *les femmes russes*, as the Russian women were called, and stereotyped, the European brothels opened their doors to Chinese as well.

The Line was notorious, but it was only a fraction of the city's sex industry. According to one estimate, the ratio of brothels to ordinary dwellings in Shanghai as a whole, including the Chinese districts, was as high as one to twelve. (In mid-19th century London, also notorious for its sex industry, the ratio had been one to sixty.) The writer Wu Zhouliu, who railed against the foreign presence in Shanghai, considered the prevalence of brothels as the result of extreme social inequality—and he blamed that inequality on European imperialism. Prostitution, Wu wrote, was 'a manifestation of a wretched desire to survive'.

When Emily began researching the topic for her novel *Miss Jill,* she asked Lorraine to introduce her to the madam of the brothel where she had worked a few years before. The house was located well away from The Line, in a quiet location on Connaught Road (now Kangding Road) in the north of the International Settlement.

In *China to Me,* the madam, a Canadian named Louise, is described as 'a large fat woman' and her British boyfriend as 'a retired and run-down Shanghai policeman'. His name was Bill, and he had served in India before moving to China and joining the Shanghai Municipal Police. Brothels were banned in the International Settlement, and so Bill was well placed to pay the bribes required by his former SMP colleagues in return for ignoring Louise's illegal establishment.

They were an utterly ordinary pair: she was fond of dachshunds and chocolate cake, he loved to talk about his time in India, and their dream was to save enough to buy a farm in Canada and retire there. Louise had been a nurse; her establishment was clean and orderly and she kept a good table for her permanent staff of prostitutes—her 'steady boarders', as she called them.

She looked out for their interests and her establishment was a far cry from the degrading hell-holes which featured in the more lurid depictions of 'white slavery'.

Outside of Emily's books, the only surviving references to the brothel are a few mentions in the correspondence between Emily and Lorraine—it's in one of these letters that Lorraine reveals that her workname there was 'Johnny Jean'. So for a broader idea of how the establishment operated we must turn to *Miss Jill,* in which the Madam is called Annette rather than Louise. The description of life in the brothel is drawn directly from Emily's research, something she confirmed in *China to Me.*

Annette brands her business 'exclusive'; which means she doesn't employ women who have worked in other Shanghai brothels. There is a distinct hierarchy among her workers, topped by the 'steady boarders'; lower in the pecking order are women who come, stay for a few weeks or so and move on. She also has casual workers on call, including a number of married women who had been introduced to her by a network of dressmakers who act as recruiters for brothel madams.

The Russian refugee women in Shanghai were known, as one Englishman put it, for their 'beauty and the ability to get things out of men'. Because they were stereotyped as immoral and grasping, Annette doesn't care to have too many of *les femmes russes* on her staff. Among her 'steady boarders' there is only one avowed Russian—but there is also a Russian who claims to be Georgian before switching to being Spanish, and other Russians who pretend to be French. There is also an American who pretends to be an Italian, but Jill is proud of her nationality and, as a good Australian abroad did in those times, she proclaims herself 'British'. She prefers British customers because she yearns to be accepted in their society.

Annette is following the industry's shift away from racial

discrimination. As customers she welcomes 'Frenchmen, British, Americans, Chinese, Indians, Japanese, Russians, Germans', and when she does exclude punters it is on the basis of class rather than race. In fact Annette's best customers are wealthy Chinese men with a preference for 'white girls', and to attract them she offers the same services as the more upmarket Chinese brothels – the 'singsong' houses.

These 'singsong' houses were more sociable institutions than their European counterparts. Wealthy Chinese men went to 'singsong' houses to dine and drink, gamble and conduct business, and one of Annette's best clients is a Chinese banker who uses the Connaught Road brothel for business entertainment 'just as if she had been a Chinese woman and her place a high-class singsong house. The fact that her cuisine was European made it all the smarter ...'.

And Jill, having lived in a Japanese household and in a geisha house, excels in the 'hostess' role at these dinners. With her 'blonde, childish prettiness and a malleability remarkable in a white girl', she is a considerable asset to the brothel, but not all of Annette's 'white girls' are as open-minded as their employer. Some show contempt for their Chinese clients by addressing them in comic pidgin English, which is understandably bad for business. Jill, however, is deferential and polite – and this seems to have been Lorraine's habit in real life.

Sir Victor Sassoon, the Shanghai plutocrat who would become Emily Hahn's lover, later recorded that Lorraine had been a favourite of the brothel's Chinese clientele. Among Lorraine's customers, Sassoon singled out Soong Tse-vung, also known as T.V. Soong, brother of the famous three Soong sisters. Together, these four siblings were among the most important members of the family clique which dominated the Republic of China – most notably the youngest sister Soong Mei-ling, who was married to

Premier Chiang Kai-Shek.

During the 1930s T.V. Soong ran his own investment bank, he held a seat on the Board of the Bank of China and he was also Chiang Kai-Shek's personal representative in Shanghai—the city from which the Kuomintang regime drew its main financial support. So at the time he was Lorraine's client, Soong was one of the wealthiest and most influential men in China and, according to the English writer Arthur Ransome who had met him some years before, he also had 'very pleasant manners, and a rather engaging confidence'. In the 1940s Soong would become even more important—as Foreign Minister and ultimately Premier of the Republic of China. With his Harvard economics degree and dubious fortune, Soong would come to embody the ambivalent relationship between the Kuomintang regime and the United States.

Because Jill attracts an elite clientele, Annette regards her as one of her star attractions. And as such, she gets special privileges in the brothel: she has the pick of the accommodation and can have meals from the excellent kitchen served in her room. Otherwise, the communal meal of the day is breakfast, served at noon, at which the 'steady boarders' pore over the society columns of the *North-China Daily News,* spotting the lies their clients have been telling them about their names and marital status. It was like checking up on someone on social media.

The newspapers also enabled Lorraine to follow the fortunes of the Tokugawa family, particularly when, in December 1935, her old friend Toyoko was married in London. Tokugawa Iemasa was now the Japanese Ambassador to Turkey and the groom's father, Matsudaira Tsueno, was Ambassador to Britain. It was a highly suitable match: soon Matsudaira would take up the position of Head of the Imperial Household Agency, which managed the Court and the Emperor's estate. Toyoko's marriage was covered in the society pages of English newspapers and magazines, and we can imagine Lorraine regaling her fellow 'steady boarders' with her connection with the Tokugawas. And later, reflecting on the gulf now separating her from her former life.

Certainly, society in the Connaught Road brothel was a step down from that Lorraine had known when she was Tokugawa's mistress. Annette has a low opinion of her workers, regarding them as too 'stupid' to look after themselves. She has to contend with heavy drinking, drug use, stealing from other workers, and – most disruptive of all – falling in love. Other occupational hazards include sexually transmitted diseases and pregnancy; in the latter case she arranges for an abortion – though she refuses to pay for the procedure, considering it the result of carelessness on the part of the worker. Suicidal gestures – a worker taking an overdose of sleeping pills in the knowledge that she will be found and a doctor summoned – are also not uncommon.

But Annette sees something in Jill, and counsels her 'to make something of herself' – to move out of the sex industry. She coaches her to select the better prospects from among her customers and give them the impression that she particularly favours them, in the hope that they will take her out of the brothel and set her up as their acknowledged mistress, or even wife.

For Jill, the most degrading part of sex work is the need to adopt an attitude of penitential submission. Sometimes, oblivious to their own role in the industry, customers in the brothel will sorrowfully ask her how a nice girl like her wound up in a place like this. She panders to their hypocrisy by making up stories to add pathos to her situation. But she grows sick of the lies which underpin her life in the brothel and ultimately it is this made-up identity of a sex worker, as much as the work itself, that she rejects.

Midway through Lorraine's time in the brothel, Emily Hahn arrived in Shanghai. And when the two women met the following year, this would prove to be a stroke of life-changing good fortune for Lorraine.

Born in St Louis Missouri, Emily had an edgy streak which showed early: at the age of 19 and dressed as a man, she and a female friend drove across America. She finished a degree in mining engineering because she was told that as a woman she couldn't, but then rejected the macho industry and took a series of casual jobs, including as a tour guide in New Mexico. There Emily met the free-spirited, bisexual patron of the arts Mabel Luhan; in the 1970s, she would write Luhan's biography. Next, Emily moved to New York and drifted into journalism. She published her first piece in *The New Yorker* in 1929, and her last would appear in 1995. Her journalistic career thus spanned the period from the Wall Street Crash to the Clinton Presidency.

Emily was writing about the sexual exploitation of women well before she was drawn to Lorraine's life as a subject. In the early 1930s she travelled across central Africa, an experience which prompted her to write a novel whose African heroine Mawa is the concubine of a white settler. Then in 1933, Emily began an affair with screenwriter Edwin Mayer; it lasted two years, but he was married and it didn't work out. However, this exposure to Hollywood contributed to her education as an author, deepening her insight into a popular culture in which the nexus between novels and movies was arguably stronger that it is today.

When she and Mayer broke up, Emily took a cruise which stopped over in Shanghai. Like Lorraine, she had just intended to pass through, but on her arrival she began an affair with Sir

Victor Sassoon and, like Lorraine, she wound up staying for years.

By now Emily had developed a distinctive voice which was in parts cynical, critical and self-aware: 'I am a young American woman with well-arranged pre-conceived ideas of Women's Rights, I took it for granted that I would find the women of China downtrodden. As it turns out, I was quite correct ...'.

This subversive tone shaded into her life as well. One of her signature quirks was a liking for monkeys and apes; she kept them as pets and took them to dinner parties dressed in dinner suits. She delighted in scandalising respectable audiences: once, as a dinner guest on board a Royal Navy warship during the crisis over the abdication of Edward VIII, she proposed a toast to her fellow American Wallis Simpson, for whom the king had just scandalously renounced the throne. (Mrs Simpson had lived in China in 1924/25, during which time, it was said, she had visited brothels in Shanghai.) A chilly silence descended on the wardroom.

Then, following her affair with Sir Victor Sassoon, Emily embarked on a relationship with the poet Shao Xunmei. She would marry Shao according to Chinese custom—as he was already married, she was formally his secondary wife—and their union had no standing in the eyes of Western officials. Emily mined their relationship and his family life for stories that she turned into articles for *The New Yorker*, stories which would later be collected and published in book form under the title *Mr Pan*. Emily was ruthless and unapologetic about this aspect of the writer's trade: as she put it: 'I use people ... People who mind should stay away from writers'.

For all that Emily was her best friend, Lorraine would come to feel the force of those words.

III

Dee Dee

There was a man in town, a wealthy broker, who was eccentric ...

Emily Hahn, *China to Me*

Just as Lorraine left no account of how she became a sex worker, neither did she leave one of why she quit the brothel. All we know is that when Lorraine did leave Madame Louise's in early 1936, she was supported to do so by the man Emily referred to as Dee Dee. His real name was Edmund Ellis Toeg, and this was the first instance of the crucial role he would play in Lorraine's life. For just as Emily would help Lorraine to accept herself, Edmund would help her to be accepted by society. He became her bridge to respectability.

In *China to Me* Edmund is a mild gentleman, always in the background, who acts almost as Lorraine's guardian and meekly bears the brunt of her foul temper. In *Miss Jill* we see another side to him: he is an Iraqi called 'Andy', a 'stubborn bachelor' and haunter of brothels where he acts out his strange fantasies. For her part, Lorraine called him Dee Dee (prompted by his initials E E) and he called her Wunsy, and these baby-talk nicknames became their signature as a couple: only their closest friends were entitled to use them and Lorraine jealously policed this privilege.

Dee Dee belonged to Wunsy, and Wunsy would define Lorraine almost as much as her family nickname Rainee did.

These were more than just everyday endearments. At a deeper level, the nicknames referred to characters in an erotic role-playing game which Lorraine dubbed the 'Wunsy, Dee Dee set up' which was at the core of their relationship. Emily, from whom Lorraine kept no secrets, described this game as something 'straight out of Victorian melodrama'. Wunsy was 'a virgin ... shy, inarticulate, ashamed, lisping' and Dee Dee her ardent, impetuous suitor—who, however, always stopped short of consummating his desire. In fact, it seems that penetrative intercourse was almost entirely absent from their relationship. Lorraine enjoyed this fantasy, remarking to Emily 'I like being Wunsy ... it's an escape from reality just like being an actress of sorts.'

In contrast to Lorraine's many surviving letters and Emily's many books, Edmund has left little in the way of written records behind him. But he was an artist, and tens of his drawings, cartoons and paintings in a variety of media—pencil, water colours and oil paintings—survive. Lorraine's nephews and nieces remember the wonderful cartoon stories that Edmund drew, featuring the pet dogs that he and Lorraine doted on. His affinity for horses shows in his hunting, polo and racing scenes. But his favourite subjects were young women—'both draped and undraped', as Lorraine put it.

And his fantasy of Wunsy was obsessively elaborated in drawings of a girlish and undraped Lorraine.

The Toegs were one of an enterprising group of families who emigrated from Ottoman Iraq in the 19th century. This community is sometimes described as 'Baghdadis' and sometimes as 'Indo-

Iraqis', and they belonged to the Sephardic branch of Judaism. The most famous of Shanghai's Sephardic families were the Sassoons, 'the Rothschilds of the East', and during Lorraine's time in the city the clan was headed by the flamboyant tycoon Sir Victor Sassoon, Emily Hahn's sometime lover, and who would become a significant figure in Lorraine's life.

In 1832, the Sassoon patriarch opened an office in Mumbai, and from there the family business spread west and east along Britain's trade routes. In Britain, the Sassoons' great success and phenomenal wealth enabled them to surmount the barriers by which Victorian society excluded outsiders. On the other side of the world, a Sassoon was credited with being the first Jew to reach modern Shanghai, and the family similarly prospered in China. They drew their business and marriage partners from among the tight-knit Baghdadi community, and this was how Edmund's father Raymond Toeg got his start. Born in Baghdad, Raymond worked for the Sassoons in Malaya and Hong Kong before setting up on his own account as a foreign exchange and bullion broker in Shanghai. Edmund's mother Sophia had a Sassoon grandmother, and Raymond and Sophia's children were Sir Victor's cousins.

By the 1930s, the Sephardic community in Shanghai numbered about one thousand, and the wealthy Sassoons and Toegs enjoyed the same kind of elite status as did their cousins in England. The more overtly racist Shanghailanders might make comments about 'Baghdad camel drivers' but, as was said of Sir Victor, one could not very well snub a man who—as he did—played golf with the Prince of Wales.

The four Toeg children—Nora, Edmund, David and Dora—were raised in a world of wealth and privilege. Later, when she was delving into the family history, Lorraine would record that the family mansion in Shanghai's Western District had been 'like a palace ... They had a staff of 30 gardeners & their own Tailor – chauffeurs, amah, headcook, undercook, butlers, etc. ... at the racecourse kept their stables with grooms etc ... nearly every year or second year (*Edmund's parents*) stayed at Monte Carlo'.

And yet, despite the Toeg's considerable standing and their Sassoon connection, Edmund's Iraqi and Jewish background meant that he would never be free of anxiety about being accepted – whether by English society or Australian immigration officials. The fear of exclusion was something he and Lorraine had in common.

Born in Shanghai in 1895, Edmund spent his early years in the family mansion on Yu Yuen (now Yuyuan) Road. In order to smooth their entry to good society, Raymond and Sophia decided to provide their children with an elite European education and so, when Edmund was eleven, Sophia moved the children to England. She bought a house outside Brighton to serve as a family home while the children completed their schooling. His teenage years in England made Edmund, culturally, an Edwardian gentleman – 'a great stickler for the old school tie & tradition' – an outlook that stayed with him all his life. He was often in the grand London homes of cousins such as Reginald Sassoon, who would become his best friend. He went to Oxford University, where he studied classics. There is no record of him having served in the First World War.

We have only occasional glimpses of Edmund in his twenties and thirties. He undertook a three-year apprenticeship in the Hongkong & Shanghai Bank before joining his father in the family brokerage firm of Toeg & Company. He travelled on business between Shanghai and London, and spent some time in the United States. It was during these years that Edmund –

like his cousins Reginald and Sir Victor Sassoon—acquired the reputation of being a wealthy playboy. One surviving fragment attests to his nightlife: a postcard sent from Frank Sebastian's New Cotton Club, a famous speakeasy and jazz club in Los Angeles (Louis Armstrong was arrested for smoking weed in the parking lot). Among the favourite subjects of Edmund's watercolour sketches were naked showgirls, and the postcard's senders—'Roses' and 'Hilda'—ardently wish that Edmund was back in L.A. so that he could continue to draw his 'cute pictures of the chorus girls'.

Otherwise, he flourished in his father's profession of foreign exchange broker. He was in the right place: trading, like transactional sex, was a Shanghai obsession. In the mid-Thirties Edmund made friends with the Reuters reporter Edward Ward, who commented that:

> *Everybody, women as well as men, talked incessantly of stocks and shares, of taking a forward position in silver, of selling sterling short, of buying a thousand bales of October Liverpool cotton and selling a load of Chicago rye. The Shanghai Gold Bar Exchange was the nearest thing I ever saw to a madhouse ...*

To buttress their social position, the Toegs immersed themselves in the sporting rituals of the Shanghailanders. These were the basis of the family's friendship with Maurice Springfield, a senior officer in the Shanghai Municipal Police and a keen amateur jockey. The connection began when Edmund's father, rich enough to keep a whole stable of racehorses, asked the policeman to ride for him at race meetings. It continued down to the 1960s when Springfield, now retired in England, published a memoir to which Edmund contributed some drawings. This memoir was entitled *Hunting Opium and other Scents* because Springfield served as head of the SMP's Narcotics Squad.

Located in the centre of the International Settlement, the Shanghai Racecourse – now People's Park – was the setting for much of Springfield's sporting career. He describes it as 'the centre of social life' – by which of course he meant *European* social life, as the club rules banned Chinese from owning racehorses. To Springfield and his ilk, sport was a way of displaying racial superiority, a justification for colonial rule. This was spelt out in a candid passage in the memoir: growing up in late Victorian Britain, Springfield and his peers had been taught:

> *to play hard, to ride straight, and above all, to enjoy ourselves in the open air. It was also taken for granted that we should thus be qualified in due course to go overseas as sailors or soldiers in the British Forces, or as administrators of the British Empire.*

Shanghai's rural hinterland was the setting for the Paper Hunt, a regular cross-country race following a paper trail through the fields. The race involved frequent clashes with enraged farmers whose crops had been trampled – confrontations which, in Springfield's eyes, only added to the fun. Edmund was a keen member of the Paper Hunt, and drew the illustrations for the Club history.

When they were not riding horses or playing cricket, the city's colonial elite were shooting wetland birds, and to get around the riverine hinterland they used another Shanghailander institution: the houseboat. Edmund named his houseboat the *Nora* after his elder sister, and in peaceful times he moored it in the Huangpu River upstream from Shanghai. He has left a beautifully illustrated diary of one excursion on the *Nora,* on which he was accompanied by Geoffrey Fitzgerald, whom he had met when they were both working for the Hongkong & Shanghai Bank. Their friendship illustrates the social web that defined the Shanghai elite.

Family links were crucial. Geoffrey Fitzgerald came from an aristocratic Irish clan and his cousin Derek Fitzgerald had married Violet Sassoon, who was Edmund's cousin and the sister of his great friend Reginald Sassoon. Sport was the religion they all worshipped: Reginald Sassoon was killed in a horse race, which earned him a eulogy from his fellow jockey, the hard-riding policeman Maurice Springfield. And money was the glue which bound them together: Derek Fitzgerald became a director of the firm of E.D. Sassoon & Co – which was owned by Sir Victor Sassoon, also Edmund's cousin. These ties endured for decades: Edmund would remain close to Geoffrey Fitzgerald, Maurice Springfield and Victor Sassoon into the 1960s.

This was the world from which Lorraine was excluded because she had been a prostitute. A decade later, when she married Edmund, she would join it.

It took a long time for Lorraine to put her time in the brothel behind her. Like her mother before her – if for somewhat different reasons – she was stalked by the fear of being exposed and shamed; Edmund, describing her state of mind to Emily, said she imagined 'that people are talking about her'. And while leaving Madam Louise's solved one problem, it created others. As Emily put it, although Edmund 'loved her deeply' he 'couldn't marry her ... he could see for himself that it wouldn't work out, not in a small place like Shanghai'.

By a 'small place' Emily meant a small foreign community; Shanghai was a megacity, but its European population was only that of a medium sized town, and within this relatively small circle the Toeg family occupied a prominent position. By now Edmund's father was dead, but his mother Sophia was a respected member of the British Womens' Association, the Jewish Communal Association of Shanghai and the Shanghai Zionist Association. His sister Nora worked as a volunteer for the Shanghai Jewish School and the other, Dora, had married the Greek Consul General, before moving with him to Athens. It would have been impossible for Edmund to marry 'Johnny Jean of Connaught Road' without jeopardising their standing.

But there was another, less obvious, reason why Edmund was reluctant to put his relationship with Lorraine on a more permanent footing: he was deeply sexually inhibited. As we have noted, it seems that he and Lorraine very rarely had actual intercourse, if at all. In a letter Lorraine wrote to Emily in 1949 she complains about Edmund's lack of interest in 'normal' sex, saying that it was the result of a complex he had suffered from 'all his life'. He had told her that the reason why he had remained unmarried until his early fifties was because he regarded himself as sexually inadequate and believed this would ruin any marriage he entered into.

So in this first phase of their relationship Lorraine was socially unacceptable as a wife while Edmund was sexually inadequate as a husband. What, then, were his plans for her? According to Emily, he wanted her to be 'a good girl, and happy'. Edmund's priority was to stop her drifting back to prostitution – a real possibility, as other madams were vying to recruit the renowned 'Johnny Jean' for their own brothels. To keep her out of the industry he paid Lorraine a regular allowance, and other expenses as they arose. Next, Edmund wanted her to qualify as a stenographer typist, so that she could earn a 'respectable' living. He wanted her to be accepted by her peers, and finally, he wanted to do 'the right thing ... but by proxy': to see her married to some suitable man of 'the protected upper classes'.

We can only guess at how Lorraine accounted to her mother for the time she spent in the sex industry. When Laura first found out that her daughter had decided to stay in Shanghai, she must have been worried. She may have insisted that Lorraine return home; perhaps they argued, perhaps Lorraine cut off or cut back contact with her mother to a bare minimum. The earliest of Lorraine's surviving letters to Laura is dated September 1937 and their subsequent correspondence sheds no light on their relations over the five years prior to that, so it's an open question just how much Laura ever came to know of her daughter's experiences. But it was enough that, when Lorraine did return to Sydney, the merest allusion to her way of life in Shanghai could reduce her mother to tears.

Laura, meanwhile, had started a new life of her own: she had moved back to Sydney and got married—her husband, Charles Glanville, was a surveyor's assistant and a decorated Gallipoli veteran. So after two decades of agonising over being an unwed mother, Laura was now respectable—although her habit of lying about her past persisted, and for some reason she found it necessary to falsify her birth details in the marriage register. And then in March 1937, her former lover Ben Chaffey died: his death broke the seal of secrecy and Laura unburdened herself to her son Peter. Fifty years later, Peter recalled how she had broken down and told him that his supposed father 'Chester Murray' had been invented to shield her children from the stigma of illegitimacy. Laura's taboo on discussing her secret life had been lifted—at least with her eldest son.

Chaffey, we recall, was not Lorraine's father, and we don't know whether Laura ever told her eldest daughter that not only was she illegitimate, but that she had a different father to her siblings. The traumas of Lorraine's childhood—the periodic exclusions from the family home—must have branded her with the awareness that she was different. But feeling is different to knowing, and this is another of Lorraine's mysteries.

Then in April 1937, Lorraine made her first trip outside China in nearly four years, travelling to England, Edmund paying for a First Class ticket. The evidence is scant, but it seems that Laura also visited London around that time, and if mother and daughter had been estranged, then they were now reconciled. Their relationship would remain volatile for years and Lorraine could be scathing about Laura. But from now on they stayed in touch.

London was celebrating the coronation of George VI. Many Australians, including politicians and socialites, had travelled to the imperial capital for the occasion and Lorraine met several of these, including a young woman named Barbara Davies. As a budding ornament of Sydney society—such as Lorraine might have been had things turned out otherwise—Davies was invited to a royal garden party at which, according to a report in the Australian press, she looked 'fresh and delightful in a pale tea rose organdie redingote worn over a matching satin slip and with a pale corn coloured hat'. This was the kind of social recognition that Lorraine craved, and envy of Davies sank into her soul.

IV

The Battle of Shanghai

We could see these horrible, great glowing masses and the sky covered with black smoke

Emily Hahn, *China to Me*

While Lorraine had been leading the pampered life of an ambassador's mistress and then a high class courtesan, the world had been sliding into what historians have dubbed the 'dark valley' of the 1930s. In the years since she had left Australia, the Great Depression had wreaked hardship on millions, the Nazis had come to power in Germany, Fascist Italy had invaded Ethiopia, and in Spain the Nationalists had launched a civil war against the democratic Republican government. In China itself, the Japanese had annexed Manchuria and in 1932 they had ravaged Shanghai's Chinese suburbs. Lorraine had remained unaffected by all this turmoil but now, suddenly, she found herself in the thick of it, travelling on the last leg of her return journey from London on the French warship *Dumont D'Urville*, up a Huangpu River dotted with floating bodies.

On 7 July 1937, Japanese and Chinese troops had clashed near the historic Marco Polo Bridge, southwest of Beijing. This marked the beginning of the Second Sino-Japanese War, which would continue for eight years and cause over fourteen million civilian deaths.

The first major campaign of the war was the Battle of Shanghai, and outside of China this is now largely remembered for three things. One was the heroic Chinese defence of the Four Banks, or *Sihang,* Warehouse. Another was 'Black Saturday', the accidental Chinese bombing of the International Settlement, which caused hundreds of casualties. Then there was the celebrated image of a crying baby in a railway station which had been bombed by the Japanese: taken by photojournalist H.S. Wong, this rapidly became the most viewed news photograph ever published. Just months earlier, the German *Luftwaffe,* supporting the Fascists in the Spanish Civil War, had obliterated the town of Guernica; now it was Shanghai's turn to experience the frightful effect of the new military technique of aerial bombardment.

At the beginning, Chinese government troops held the initiative around Shanghai, attacking the Japanese enclave of Hongkou. In late August and September, the Japanese countered with amphibious landings near the mouth of the Huangpu River, and by late October they had enveloped the city's northern outskirts. Then in November, the Japanese made another amphibious landing on the shores of Hangzhou Bay, to the south of the city, forcing what was left of the Chinese forces to retreat westward towards the Chinese capital Nanjing.

The Battle of Shanghai was the first time that any great city anywhere had been subjected to the unfettered use of modern weaponry, and the destruction in the city's Chinese suburbs was unprecedented. It was a foretaste of things to come. Percy Finch was an eyewitness to the carnage and as he put it—in the verbose journalese of the times—'Shanghai was the first of the world's big cities to be sacrificed to the God of Destruction who laid his calamitous hand upon the most populous section of the globe in World War II'. For the Chinese people it was a catastrophe. For

Lorraine, it was the beginning of her political education.

London had been abuzz with talk of the volunteers who had travelled to Spain to support the Republican, anti-Fascist cause in the Civil War. Perhaps this inspired Lorraine, because she volunteered to work as a nurse's aide in the International Settlement's Lester Hospital (now the Renji Hospital). And now we have reached a significant moment in her story, because it's at this point that the surviving collection of her letters begins: from now on, we can hear her own voice. In a letter to Laura she told how ...

> *...At first I was sick when I had to stand by & watch the wounded having their wounds dressed, now I can change dressings myself ... we are eating Chinese vegetables & rice & no meat ... Our windows are barricaded with sandbags, the streets are barbed-wired in case of emergencies & sandbag entrenchments with police inside, at every road crossing.*

And it is also our introduction to Lorraine the not-always-reliable narrator. Her description of life in embattled Shanghai includes colourful eyewitness accounts of 'hundreds of mutilated victims lying in compounds' and of wounded Chinese soldiers demanding to be sent back to the front line despite their missing limbs. She tells how she narrowly escaped the bomb that caused the carnage on Black Saturday—and even of being wounded herself. All of this might very well have happened, but some of it sounds like vicarious experience—for example, we never hear about her wound again. And as Emily—who knew Lorraine better than anyone—warned: 'You never knew when the mood would take her to spin tales'.

When the battle broke out, Emily had been teaching English

in a college, but this closed because of the conflict and she took a casual job teaching a Japanese man – 'probably whatever they call spies nowadays'. He was staying in the Park Hotel, Shanghai's tallest building, and the view from his room was horrifying: it seemed to her that the Chinese suburbs were engulfed in flames.

> *We could see these horrible, great glowing masses and the sky covered with black smoke, and a huge lemon-yellow moon. Three planes flew across the moon. There was a bomb in Pootung* (Pudong), *and a bigger orange flare ....*

She was now living on Yu Yuen Road in Shanghai's Western District. As the Japanese drew closer, the district became exposed to the fighting and when bombs started dropping near her house even the fearless Emily decided the war was getting too close. She moved into the French Concession, to 1826 Avenue Joffre, which would be her home for the remainder of her time in Shanghai.

It was during these weeks that Emily bumped into Lorraine and the war correspondent Luigi Barzini at Farren's nightclub.

The years of the 'dark valley' were good ones for Barzini and his peers. The Italian invasion of Ethiopia and the Spanish Civil War provided fertile ground for the romantic image of the foreign correspondent, risking their lives to bear witness to noble causes. One of Lorraine's fellow-passengers aboard the *Dumont D'Urville* had been Philip Stephens of London's *Daily Telegraph,* who had been among the first to report the bombing of Guernica; in Shanghai Stephens would come to fill that heroic mould.

The media pack covering the Battle of Shanghai based themselves in the neutral foreign enclave, a vantage point which allowed them to observe both sides of the front line and then return to their luxury hotels to write their stories. As Edgar Snow of the London *Daily Herald* observed, it was as if the great battles of the Western Front had been fought in Paris while one bank of the Seine remained neutral. Snow would go on to become arguably the most famous China-watcher of his generation. He had just completed *Red Star Over China*, a book about his visit to remote Shaanxi Province, where the Chinese communists were based. Published at the end of 1937, it would be dubbed 'the scoop of the century' because it introduced Mao Tse-tung and the Chinese Communist leadership to a world audience—and *Red Star* would become part of Lorraine's political education. Helen Foster Snow, Edgar's wife, would make her own visit to the Communist base, obtaining material for her own book *Inside Red China*.

Among the other foreign journalists in Shanghai were three who would surface later in Lorraine's life.

During the battle, Lorraine worked as a typist for the American Hubert Knickerbocker. A Pulitzer Prize winner, Knickerbocker was on the staff of the Hearst International News Service agency and among his many scoops had been an interview with Stalin's mother, which became the source of a famous story. As the journalist rose to leave, the confused old lady had asked him: 'But tell me, what does my son do for a living?' Lorraine would later regret retelling this anecdote.

The second was Harold Timperley, the Australian-born correspondent of *The Manchester Guardian*. As much activist as journalist, Timperley was part of the Chinese government propaganda network—managed by the Australian W.H. Donald—helping to mobilise international opinion against Japanese aggression.

The third was the American cameraman Norman Alley, who worked for Universal Newsreel. Alley was staying in the Cathay

Hotel, now the Peace Hotel, a tower block which stood on the Bund facing onto the Huangpu River. In his memoir *I Witness,* Alley described the daily round of the foreign press corps: breakfast at the Cathay, followed by a trip to the front line and then a viewing of the bombardment of the Chinese city from the comfortable setting of a hotel balcony, punctuated by attendance at press conferences. They drank in a nightclub called The Tower at the top of the Cathay which was, Emily noted, a favourite watering hole because of the panoramic view it gave of the 'general shooting and excitement'.

The society of these journalists dramatically broadened Lorraine's horizons. War in Europe was still two years off but, coming in the wake of the conflicts in Ethiopia and Spain, the Japanese attack on China had made the totalitarian threat unambiguously clear. Working and socializing with the Shanghai media pack, and falling in love with Barzini, Lorraine felt that she was 'watching world history being changed', and being drawn into the great geopolitical drama unfolding around her.

She wasn't alone. Everywhere people were being caught up in events, becoming politicised, and taking a stand—sometimes at odds with their own governments. Italy's Fascist regime, of which Barzini was an eloquent representative, supported Tokyo, but he would say (albeit years later) that in China, the Japanese had been 'engaged in a brutal war of aggression ... I did not enjoy defending Italy's foreign policy'. And yet in 1937, the policy of the Western democracies was not notably more principled than that of the Fascist dictatorships; fearful of offending Tokyo, Britain and the US were slow to come to China's aid, just as they had washed their hands of Ethiopia and Republican Spain. But for left-leaning liberals like Emily, Edgar and Helen Snow, Stephens and Timperley, the issue was clear: China was fighting the same battle as the Spanish republicans: for freedom, and against fascism. As Snow said: 'China was my cause'.

Amidst all this turmoil, personal loyalties came under strain. Did loyalty to one's friends and lovers take precedence over loyalty to one's country? Did loyalty to a supranational ideal, like communism, take precedence to loyalty to one's country? It was a time for commitment—but it would take a while for Lorraine to choose a side.

By now Lorraine was living in the French Concession, sharing an apartment in the Avenue du Roi Albert (now Shaanxi South Road) with a Swedish friend, Vivienne Dorf. For a while, she and Dorf were a double attraction on the frenetic Shanghai social scene. According to Lorraine, because so many civilians had been evacuated, the two were about the only young unattached foreign women left in Shanghai and they were showered with invitations to dances and cocktail parties.

The battle posed Edmund a different problem: how to protect his beloved houseboat. He had moored the *Nora* in Suzhou Creek, which partially formed the northern boundary between the International Settlement and the Chinese municipality and now, with the fighting approaching, he decided to try and protect the boat by covering it with sandbags. Suzhou Creek was virtually the front line and any Chinese labourer approaching it risked being shot, and so Edmund, his loyal Chinese boatman, Lorraine and some other friends did the job themselves. Lorraine reported in a letter home that when they reached the *Nora* they found she had been damaged: 'Many stray shells and pieces of shrapnel had pierced right through the roof'. A photo of the episode, which appeared in the Australian newspapers, shows her wearing a British infantry helmet.

By the last week of October the Japanese had almost cleared

the defenders from the north bank of Suzhou Creek. The last remaining Chinese redoubt was the Four Banks Warehouse, defended by the unit which would go down in history as 'the Eight Hundred Heroes'. On the day the final Japanese assault on the warehouse began, Norman Alley was higher up Suzhou Creek at the Jessfield Bridge, filming a flood of Chinese refugees:

> *I got a comfortable closeup of a hellish panorama. With the banzai-shouting Japanese practically at their shuffling heels, there were literally hordes upon hordes of Chinese refugees struggling frantically to get across this small railroad bridge spanning Soochow Creek ... Bombs, artillery and machine guns heckled their path as they ran the gory gauntlet. Old men and women, dead tired from fleeing, and scared to a living death. Women shouldering double-basketed bamboo poles bearing precious cargoes of babies and food.*

Among those watching the scene was General Telfer-Smollett, commander of the British troops in Shanghai. When a Chinese woman carrying her baby collapsed at the end of the bridge, Telfer-Smollett braved Japanese fire to help the woman to safety, a feat that Alley recorded in his memoir.

Meanwhile, the Japanese encirclement of the foreign enclave tightened. Lorraine had left some belongings in a house in the threatened Western District and she went out to collect them, but she miscalculated, and by the time she was ready to return the curfew had come into force. So she was trapped for the night, right where the next clash between the Japanese and Chinese forces was expected to take place. She rang up Barzini, who told her to take shelter at the back of the residence. In a letter to Laura, she told how she 'went to the garage where I found all the servants and many of their refugee relations, wives and numerous kiddies enjoying the safety of the concrete garage. I slept in the back seat of an antiquated Rolls Royce'.

The day after Lorraine wrote about her adventure, the Japanese made an amphibious landing on the shores of Hangzhou Bay and drove north, threatening to encircle the remains of the Chinese Army. A few days later, the Chinese forces withdrew from the city's environs—with the exception of those in the district of Nantao, on the southern side of the foreign enclave. There, Chinese President Chiang Kai-Shek ordered his troops to make a last-ditch defence.

On the evening of 10th November Lorraine had cocktails with Hubert Knickerbocker and Philip Stephens in the Park Hotel. The next day was Armistice Day, now known as Remembrance Day. The Allies of the First World War commemorated as they always did and Lorraine and Vivienne Dorf, invited by an Italian military attaché, attended the ceremonial parade. This was held at the Shanghai Racecourse and a unit of Italian Savoie Grenadiers, veterans of the Ethiopian campaign, took part. The fact that in Ethiopia the Italians had used chemical weapons and carried out large-scale massacres of civilians didn't diminish Lorraine's admiration for the Grenadiers, who 'looked lovely in their romantic uniforms'.

While the parade was going on, the Japanese were attacking the last pocket of Chinese resistance in Nantao, using artillery on the north side of the foreign enclave to bombard the Chinese positions to the south of it—which meant that their shells were flying right over the Racecourse. The parade over, the media pack went to observe the fighting; Phillip Stephens was watching from a vantage point inside the neutral French Concession when a Japanese machine gun fired on his position and killed him. Stephens had annoyed the Japanese by ridiculing their propaganda claims and some believed he had been deliberately targeted by the Japanese to rid themselves of an irritant. The suspicion was that he had been singled out by Horiguchi Yoshinori, a journalist who was both a correspondent for the Japanese official newsagency *Domei* and a spokesman for the Japanese Army.

The fall of Nantao marked the end of the Battle of Shanghai. 'Everything is so quiet,' Lorraine noted in a letter home. 'No shells and guns booming and planes zooming, it feels quite strange.' Now entirely surrounded by the invading Japanese, Shanghai's foreign enclave entered the last phase of its autonomous existence, dubbed the 'isolated island' (*gudao*) period. The Japanese would eventually take over the enclave after the outbreak of the Pacific War in December 1941. But in the four remaining years of its autonomous existence, this isolated island would become the setting for European Shanghai's final revels, fuelled by an economic boom, and wracked by terrorism as Chinese government agents fought it out with the Japanese and their Chinese collaborators.

V

The Luigi Period

These women were a recognised institution, but carefully fenced in by rigorous etiquette. It was embarrassing and cruel.

Luigi Barzini, *Memories of Mistresses*

When Lorraine came to look back on the men in her life, Barzini was the one she remembered most fondly. Their affair—she called it 'the Luigi Period'—only lasted a rocky six months, but what it lacked in duration, it made up for in its intensity.

In his day Barzini's father, Luigi Barzini senior, had been one of the most famous journalists in the world. He was co-driver of the winning Italian entry in the 1907 Peking-to-Paris car race, and his book about the race was translated into eleven languages. He was also an early supporter of Mussolini and he stuck with the Fascist regime to the bitter end. Barzini junior was a Fascist, too. When he was just twenty, he helped ghost write an 'autobiography' of Mussolini; then he got a job on his father's old paper, the *Corriere della Sera*. In the mid-1930s, he picked up the plum assignments for a foreign correspondent—the Italian invasion of Ethiopia, the Spanish Civil War, the Soviet Union—before joining the media pack converging on Shanghai.

Barzini was working in tandem with Sandro Sandri of *La*

Stampa, and the two were looking to extend their coverage of the war beyond the Shanghai sector, planning trips to the Chinese capital of Nanjing and to North China. Lorraine was soon included in those plans: in a letter to Laura she reported she would be accompanying Barzini as an interpreter. To add to the French she had learned at school and the Japanese she had picked up during 'the Tokugawa Period', she was now claiming competence in spoken Mandarin, Italian and Russian.

Nine days later, her plans had changed: Barzini was now going to Nanjing on his own while Lorraine accompanied Sandri and another journalist ...

> *... to North China and Manchuria to see what is happening behind Jap lines ... If General Matsui* (later executed as a war criminal for his role in the Rape of Nanjing) *gives me a pass then I will certainly go. These chaps* (Sandri and his colleague) *speak no English so I talk with them in French besides as I mentioned my Chinese and Japanese will now come in very handy. Of course the Japs just hate us English like poison but as I will be working for a friendly country as Italy they may grant me permission for this trip ...*

But the North China gig didn't eventuate. By now the Japanese were pursuing the retreating Chinese army westward to Nanjing, and Barzini, Sandri and other journalists, including Harold Timperley and Norman Alley, flocked to the city to cover the impending battle for the capital. By 11 December, the Japanese Army was at Nanjing's gates and many of the foreign media, including the two Italians, took refuge on an American gunboat, the USS *Panay*. But any sanctuary it offered proved illusory, because the next day the *Panay* was bombed and sunk by the

Japanese, with Norman Alley filming the attack from the deck of the doomed vessel.

Before video clips, before television, another visual medium played a major role in shaping public opinion about foreign conflicts: newsreels. These were short films on current affairs shown in cinemas, and they were what Norman Alley produced. Following the sinking of the *Panay*, Alley made his way back to Shanghai and from there, he and his precious film were taken by a US Navy destroyer to the Philippines, where he transferred to the new trans-Pacific air service. On 29 December, 'Only ten days and eighteen hours after I had left Shanghai!' Alley marvelled, he arrived in New York. His footage was shown to President Roosevelt and senior administration officials, and then in movie theatres all across the United States.

Alley's *Bombing of the USS Panay* influenced history. It helped start the swing in American public opinion against Japan, a swing which would culminate in Roosevelt's August 1941 embargo on oil exports to Japan – the trigger for Pearl Harbour. To capitalise on the sensation, MGM rushed into production *Too Hot to Handle*, a romcom starring Clark Gable and Myrna Loy about the adventures of newsreel cameramen in war-torn China. But not all the journalists on board the *Panay* were so lucky. Barzini's colleague Sandro Sandri was wounded in the Japanese attack and he died hours later – he appears, near death, in Alley's newsreel. In Barzini's epitaph for Sandri, he said his friend had 'died as he lived: as a soldier, as a fascist and as a journalist.'

Barzini was himself initially reported to have died in the attack on the *Panay*, but then he turned up in Shanghai looking, according to Lorraine, 'rather like a ghost nervy unshaven with a few shrapnel scratches and in a borrowed sailors overcoat as he had given his to Sandri before he died'. But their reunion was a stormy one, because a few days later Lorraine took an overdose, triggered by Barzini's less-than-supportive response when she told him that she was pregnant, and was rushed to hospital.

In the wake of her overdose, Barzini agreed to adopt the child – recognition of their relationship, but well short of the offer of marriage Lorraine might have been hoping for. In *China to Me,* Emily did not mention the pregnancy, but she did give Lorraine's account of Barzini's attempt to ditch her:

> *... there I was with my heart breaking because I never would see him again. And because he said I ought to, I started to study at business college and I was having an awful time with that terrible shorthand, and he kept telling me how much better a life it would be than I had before, working as someone's secretary and finally marrying a clerk if I was very good ... And all the while he was talking ... So I went home and took poison. I often do. Veronal.*

As Emily's light-hearted treatment of the episode shows, Lorraine's suicide attempt was taken less seriously than it would have been today. In their world, suicide and suicide attempts were common – partly because powerful barbiturates like Veronal were so freely available. As Emily put it, 'Doctors in Shanghai have to use stomach pumps a lot.'

Public discussion of the issue in general was, by today's standards, insensitive. When the Sino-Japanese War broke out, one cartoon in the *North-China Daily News* portrayed China's decision to resist Japan as the act of an attractive *qipao*-clad woman preparing to drink poison. And Emily would later publish a short story in *The New Yorker* in which a character, recognisably Lorraine, is dubbed 'The Girl Who Commits Suicide' because of her repeated attention-seeking suicidal gestures. If this seems callous, Emily's attitude also involved a degree of self-recognition because some years earlier, going through emotional turmoil in New York, she herself had taken an overdose.

In early January 1938, Barzini travelled to Hong Kong; Lorraine joined him and while there, she terminated her pregnancy. By the end of the month, she was back in Shanghai, writing a cheery letter to Laura, dismissing the episode which had landed her in hospital over Christmas as 'slight nervous strain'—a standard 1930s euphemism for a mental health crisis. An Italian cruiser, the *Raimondo Montecuccoli*, had been visiting Shanghai at the time; Barzini had organised the officers to visit Lorraine in hospital and they had filled 'her room with flowers'. Barzini 'been a great help to me', she continued, 'and he said if ever I was in need of anything to always look on him as an elder brother'. But not, it was clear, as a husband.

Edmund had welcomed Lorraine's affair with Barzini, as it was consistent with his hopes for her to mix in normal society and, for his part, the Italian had treated Edmund as Lorraine's guardian, with courteous deference. But now, in the wake of her overdose, Edmund once more approached Emily seeking her help on Lorraine's behalf. The first time he had simply asked her to hold a party for Lorraine to introduce her to women of her own age. This time he had a much bigger favour to ask: for Emily to take Lorraine under her wing, to 'educate' her and 'fix her up until someone else married her'. And so Lorraine moved into Emily's house in the Avenue Joffre.

We next hear of Lorraine in early March, when she wrote to Emily from Beijing. She and Barzini were living in the Grand Hotel de Pekin, where foreigners with any pretensions to status stayed. But since the Japanese occupation of the Beijing region six months before, Europeans had left the city 'in droves' and there were only few staying at the hotel. The remaining guests were 'all Japs Colonels and other army and businessmen'.

Lorraine addresses her new best friend by her nickname of 'Mickey', and the letter echoes Emily's own pert style. But despite its breezy tone, it is clear that Lorraine's affair with Barzini is not going well, and that he is trying to brush her off. She is staying in his hotel room, but mentions as a significant detail that they sleep in separate beds.

Years later, when he came to write his essay 'Memories of Mistresses', Barzini criticised the way Italian society excluded such women through a 'cruel' code of etiquette. But during their time together in Beijing, he himself applied that same 'rigorous' code to his treatment of Lorraine. When he moved from the hotel to a rented house, Barzini agreed to Lorraine moving in with him – on condition that she hid herself away when he had visitors. This did little to soothe Lorraine's chronic anxiety about social acceptance, which was flaring up after she had been snubbed by the English community in Beijing. One Englishwoman, she told Emily, had 'been making pointed remarks about me... by now the whole of the community suspects our relationship (*i.e. that she was Barzini's mistress*) and I have had no further invitations from the women'.

On the other hand, Barzini had brought Lorraine back into the orbit of the Catholic Church:

> *Luigi had become intensely religious I don't know whether it is something in this northern atmosphere. He has been dining with Apostolic delegates and priests and last night he said I really should go to confession as it is not good to let sins accumulate especially after what I had*

> *gone through* (perhaps a reference to her abortion) ... *I found he had already spoken to a priest about me and had made an appointment for next Friday for me to make my confession and then on Sunday I would be able to attend Holy Communion ... Oh Emily, just see what I am prepared to go through for love (by the way I am madly in love again with him) ...*

The best part of this letter is Lorraine's description of a ceremony that she witnessed at the Temple of Confucius, in which high government officials assembled to pay their respects to the sage. This ancient ceremony, which had been in abeyance since the end of the Empire in 1911, had now been revived by the Japanese puppet regime based in Beijing. Arriving before dawn in the freezing dark, she and Barzini watched as

> *... a priest came out on the dais in a marvellous robe and beat the gong .... first the beating was slow and then the tempo grew faster and faster until I felt a cold wind go right through me ... the priests chanted from inside the temple to the accompaniment of music made on a very old type of instruments I think they were some kind of wind instruments and gongs and bells. It was so weird and beautiful and entirely different to the Chinese music of this day ...*

By late April, Barzini's rejection of Lorraine was nearly final. He had been away on a reporting tour of the battlefront, and during his absence Lorraine had suffered a health crisis. Starting to haemorrhage, she had been treated by the Italian Legation's Dr Capuzzo, who said the bleeding was the result of her recent abortion. Lorraine's description of Capuzzo as 'a darling' will surprise readers of Paul French's bestseller *Midnight in Peking,* which implicates him in the brutal murder of the young British woman Pamela Werner the previous year.

When Barzini returned, he proved even less supportive than before, and Lorraine moved back to the Grand Hotel. But despite this cooling in their relations, Italians in general had now become some of her favourite people. 'Do not think that I have Italian and foreign friends because of some romantic notion,' she wrote to Laura, 'it just happens that my friends among those nationalities are cleverer and have all round qualities which I have rarely found in Anglo Saxons'. (We will hear this note of disdain for her own kind—particularly for Australian men—again.) Among the other Italian friends she made at this time was the diplomat Franco Farinacci who worked in the Italian Consulate in Shanghai; in later years Lorraine often referred to Farinacci in the same breath as she did Barzini, which suggests that they too may have been lovers.

And now the Italian community in Beijing came to her rescue: one of the Legation staff offered to throw a party for her, a gesture which she saw as a riposte to the English society dragons who had snubbed her. The *simpatico* Italians even came up with a long term solution to Lorraine's predicament: that she should marry the Frenchman Monsieur Bardac, a long-term Beijing resident. Barzini endorsed the suggestion, but Lorraine rejected it because, as she told Emily, the prospect of marriage to Bardac was 'oh so boring'.

And then she delivered the line which, while it was just a throwaway, could stand as a motto for her time in China—and for several years thereafter:

'One has much more fun when demimonde'.

'The Luigi Period' petered out amidst unseemly differences over money. Lorraine couldn't pay her bill at the Grand Hotel and Barzini positively refused to do so, having spent all his money on Chinese antiques. Moreover, though it's not quite clear why this was part of the financial equation, he was looking after Lorraine's dog Jaime—who, incredibly, would survive World War II and re-surface in Europe a decade later. Barzini insisted that Edmund should pay Lorraine's hotel bill but she, feeling guilty about asking Edmund for yet more money, couldn't bring herself to raise the subject with him. And so she deputed Emily to ask Edmund for the money on her behalf:

> *Luigi has just been here & said that as he is looking after my welfare (I suppose spiritually as I notice there is nothing financial about it) & he must consider me as a sister & he wants me to get married before he leaves China ... everything now depends on poor Dee Dee & I'm sure I don't want to marry M. Bardac. I'd much rather have his money & go to Europe later on & meet somebody rich & I'd might be able to have a handsome Italian lover if I had money ...*

And on this wistful note, the record of the Luigi Period comes to an end. Lorraine returned to Shanghai, and settled back in with Emily; Barzini stayed on in North China and went back to Europe at the end of 1938.

Ultimately, there were no hard feelings.

VI

Life in the Isolated Island

I just didn't want to learn stenography

Shanghai bar hostess

Lorraine shared Emily's house in the Avenue Joffre for much of 1938, and the portrait of Jean in *China to Me* records the impression that Lorraine made at the time.

The first thing that struck people was her appearance. Emily said that Lorraine was 'one of the most beautiful women I have ever seen', and we can see why in a studio portrait taken around this time, showing her swathed in one of her prized furs, looking coolly over her shoulder: with her high arched eyebrows, she could be channelling the Hollywood star Jean Harlow: she is proudly, disdainfully exquisite.

It's in *China to Me* that we first hear that Lorraine had relationships – sexual relationships – with women. As Emily put it, when there were no men around to fall in love with, Lorraine 'fell in love with women' – and her praise of Lorraine's beauty is fulsome enough to make one wonder whether she herself felt the attraction. After all, Emily had previously moved in gay and bisexual circles – like Mabel McLuhan's – and this was the era of Hollywood's famed 'Sewing Circle' of bisexual women – including Marlene Dietrich, star of the hit movie *Shanghai Express*.

This is the background to a story Emily tells about Lorraine and a Russian woman called Selma. She begins by invoking the stereotype of *les femmes russes*: Russian women are 'full of sex appeal', magnets for male attention and consequently 'the American and French and English and German women of Shanghai hate them like poison'. Selma, Emily wrote, 'was one of those Russians you hear about ... you could have found out all sorts of things about her which wouldn't sound well in a drawing room ...'

Lorraine is in love with Selma, but their relationship is fraught with rivalry. Because of her past as a prostitute Lorraine considers herself an outcast, but Selma, who 'had been a bad girl too', is not only accepted in society but taunts Lorraine with the fact. On one occasion Selma is invited by Sir Victor Sassoon to join his party at the Racecourse; she tells Lorraine that she had urged Sir Victor to invite her as well, but he had refused because he 'didn't think it would be fair to his other guests ... to introduce the ladies to a girl who – well, who used to be a prostitute'. Lorraine's reaction to this humiliation is to take another overdose of Veronal.

Another undertone in Emily's house was espionage.

Emily may have flaunted her disregard for convention, but compared to the American journalist Agnes Smedley she was tame. A passionate communist, Smedley reviled the lifestyle of hyper-capitalist Shanghai's wealthy European and Chinese populations as a 'life-destroying plague' and though her precise affiliations with Soviet intelligence and the Chinese Communist Party (CCP) are obscure, she worked hard for both organisations. In the early 1930s, the Soviet masterspy Richard Sorge had been based in Shanghai and Smedley had become both his fellow-agent and lover. It was she who introduced Sorge to Ursula Kuczynski, whom he recruited and who, as 'Agent Sonya', would go on to become one of the most celebrated spies of her generation.

At the time Emily met her, Smedley was working for Soong Ching-ling, the second of the three Soong sisters. In marked contrast to her right-wing siblings, who stood at the head of the Kuomintang regime, Soong Ching-ling supported the CCP. In February 1937, Smedley had travelled to the CCP's headquarters in their 'liberated zone' in Yan'an, where she lived alongside the Party's leaders, including Mao Tse-tung. The CCP's underground network in Shanghai was under close surveillance from both Chinese and European intelligence agencies. And so Smedley, to reduce the risk of her letters from Yan'an being intercepted by the authorities, asked her friend Emily—well-connected and a relative political cleanskin—to allow her home to be used as a forwarding address. Emily agreed. At this time, she was herself leaning towards communism because, as she later explained, the liberal Western intelligentsia to which she belonged 'approved of Russia, so I did too'. (Here she was using 'Russia' as a generic term for the international communist movement, including the CCP.) As it happened, at least one of Smedley's clandestine letters routed through Emily's address was intercepted—apparently with no adverse consequences.

Emily didn't just help communists. Following the Battle of Shanghai, at the request of her Chinese husband Shao Xunmei, she hosted a clandestine radio transmitter in her home in the Avenue Joffre. This was operated by the *Juntong*, the Chinese government's intelligence service, and it was a risky business: the authorities were on the lookout for such illegal radios because they compromised the neutrality of the foreign enclave. The Japanese Army operated radio direction finding equipment around the boundary of the enclave and could calculate the approximate location of such transmitters. They could then protest to the foreign authorities, which might prompt a search of the area. After a visit from the police Emily got rattled, and asked the radio crew to leave, and it was Lorraine who moved into the vacated 'transmitter room'.

Opium was another undertone. Shao Xunmei had introduced Emily to the habit and by 1938 she was becoming dependent on the drug. Years later, Lorraine would recall how 'when I lived with Emily Hahn in Shanghai I used to smoke opium. She was married to Sin May (Shao Xunmei)—I used to make the opium pipes, because Sin May taught me and I had a good touch at fixing the pipes... I long since broke the habit'.

Despite this unconventional milieu, Edmund regarded Emily as a good influence. Partly this was because eligible men flocked to Emily's house, and so Lorraine was well placed to meet a potential husband there. So he kept on paying her allowance—conditional on her staying away from sex work. And on attending stenography courses.

At this time, the idea that stenography offered women a way to respectable self-sufficiency was a staple of popular culture. But though a commonplace of books and movies, the occupation was no miracle cure for inequality. The pay was notoriously low: Lorraine's fictional avatar Jill, struggling to learn shorthand, reflects bitterly that even if she succeeds it would take her a week's work as a typist to earn as much as she could make in a few hours in the brothel. And because so many typists were needy young women they were often seen as being either easy to exploit or promiscuous. This tension between the prospect of independence and the reality of subservience was brilliantly depicted in the 1932 Hollywood classic *Grand Hotel*, where the 'little stenographess' Flaemmchen, played by Joan Crawford, confronts the men who proposition her with the injustice of the power imbalance between them.

In her writings of this period, Emily sometimes seems almost as interested in stenography as she is in prostitution, and in fact there was a link: living in New York during the Depression, she had seen a lot of unemployed typists reduced to prostitution. As a result Emily was inclined to think that in pinning her hopes on stenography as a way back into mainstream society Lorraine—and Edmund and Barzini, who were urging her along—were being led astray by a Hollywood cliché. In *China to Me,* she noted that Lorraine had picked up the idea from a movie and that 'she started learning shorthand on an average of four times a year, whenever some earnest young man had a good long talk with her and persuaded her to reform'.

But however sceptical about stenography as the means, Emily was always quite clear about the end: Lorraine needed to give up not just prostitution but her demimondaine lifestyle altogether. Whatever form it took, regular employment would be her path to economic independence and self-respect.

In *China to Me,* Emily portrays herself as a kind of cool agony aunt who guides the 'flibbertigibbet' Jean through the 'mess of her affairs'. But her welcoming of Lorraine into her home was not entirely disinterested: she hoped her new housemate would make a good subject for a novel. And so, when Lorraine had settled in 'we soon set to work... This entailed long conversations about everyone in town who had ever visited her at Louise's...'

Lorraine was happy to talk to Emily about her experiences, but that didn't mean she had conquered her fear of being outed as a former prostitute. From time to time, one of Emily's gentlemen callers would turn out to be a former client of Lorraine's, and when this happened

> *she rushed into my bedroom to whisper hoarsely, "that man downstairs – I know him!" I would say, "Well, never mind. Come on down," and down we went, and I would duly note the start of surprise, the amazed expression on my guest's face as I introduced him. I liked it. So did Jean, sitting demurely in a corner.*

As part of the research for the novel the two women visited Lorraine's old workplace, so that Emily could garner background detail. For the occasion, Emily posed as a deserted wife seeking employment in the brothel – a lurid touch insisted on by Lorraine, who always 'preferred telling a lie if it was a good one'. Emily was surprised by the décor at Connaught Road, approving its 'spare, chaste, modern style'. She was even more surprised by Louise, who was quite unlike 'the sort of madam you read about'. (She may have had in mind Miss Reba, the beer-swilling madam in William Faulkner's bestselling novel *Sanctuary*, which had recently been made into a sensational movie.) Louise, it turned out, was 'a comfortable, chatty, woman who deplored bad language and dirty jokes'; she offered the visitors tea and some of her famous chocolate cake.

The only louche note was the 'appraising manner' in which Louise's Chinese houseboy looked at Emily. Lorraine explained that he was in fact a mainstay of the business, and always on the lookout for new recruits to work at the brothel, particularly as the supply of European women had dried up since the outbreak of the Sino-Japanese war. Emily's cover as a job applicant proved all too convincing and for some time after their visit Madam Louise harassed her with offers of employment.

It was around this time that Emily first met Charles Boxer, the British military intelligence officer she would later marry. Boxer was based in Hong Kong and, intrigued by some book reviews

Emily had written, he decided to call on her when next visiting Shanghai. Later he recalled how, on arrival at 1826 Avenue Joffre, he was shown into her living room and while he was waiting for Emily to appear, her pet gibbon decided to investigate...

> *I heard someone on the steps, and I turned around and held out my hand, saying, 'Oh, Miss Hahn?' And an enormous ape came down, wearing a red cap. It wasn't just what I was expecting. He swung around the curtains and stared at me until I was quite nervous, and then you came down and after that some blonde woman followed you up. Extraordinarily pretty she was. She sat in the corner and stared at me all the time I was speaking.*

The 'extraordinarily pretty' woman was Lorraine, and being present at their very first meeting meant she would always be a part of Emily's and Charles' inner circle.

The year 1938 was one of the most terrible in modern Chinese history. Following their capture of the Chinese capital, the Japanese had carried out the massacre which came to be known as the 'Rape of Nanking'—Harold Timperley was one of the first Western journalists to report the atrocity. Nevertheless for Shanghailanders it was largely a time of business and pleasure as usual. The writer J.G. Ballard, who grew up in Shanghai, recalled that life in the International Settlement was unaffected by the months of fighting around the city:

> *as if the bitter warfare had been little more than a peripheral entertainment of a particularly brutal kind. The neon signs shone ever more brightly over Shanghai's four hundred*

nightclubs, the bars and dance halls were filled with Number 2 and Number 3 girls, and the roulette wheels turned in the casinos, spinning their dreams of old Shanghai.

The war drove a wave of refugees into the foreign enclave, trebling its population. Percy Finch recorded that 'tens of thousands simply made the streets their homes, sleeping anywhere at night, sitting or wandering aimlessly during days', and he noted that over 100,000 corpses had been collected off the streets of the International Settlement during the first year of the war alone. But alongside this humanitarian disaster, an influx of capital and relocation of businesses to the safe-haven of the foreign enclave had triggered a dramatic economic boom. Shanghai had always been a byword for inequality, but now the gap between rich and poor became more blatant than ever before.

Not all the refugees flooding into the city were Chinese. Throughout 1938, intensifying Nazi repression prompted an exodus from Germany and Austria and, because of its relaxed entry controls, foreign-controlled Shanghai became a haven for them: eventually some twenty thousand European Jews would find refuge there. One refugee who had arrived in the city some time before was Walter Fuchs, who had worked in the German Consulate until he was sacked because of his part-Jewish ancestry. Fuchs was also gay, which made him doubly a target of the Nazis. To make ends meet, Fuchs took to teaching German and for a while Lorraine and Emily took lessons as a way of offering him support.

Another German refugee was Horst Reihmer, the proprietor of a bar called the Maskee (maskee being a pidgin term for 'don't worry'). With its clientele of refugees, demimondaines and spooks, the Maskee sounds like a Shanghai version of Rick's Café in *Casablanca*. It became one of Emily's favourite nightspots—'a nice little place', she called it—and Lorraine worked there as a hostess. But the British authorities identified Reihmer as an informant for Nazi intelligence and so her association with the Maskee told against her, becoming another black mark on her security record.

The Austrian artist Friedrich Schiff was another regular, and he memorialised the milieu in a book of cartoons called *Maskee – A Shanghai Sketchbook*. One of these shows a blonde bar girl chatting to an American sailor who has asked her a standard question like 'What's a nice girl like you doing in a place like this?' — to which she replies 'I just didn't want to learn stenography'. There's just a chance this cartoon is actually a portrait of Lorraine herself—and if it's not, it shows the extent to which the typist's dilemma, the choice between unappealing low paid office work and pandering to male desire, loomed over the lives of her and her peers.

The largest foreign refugee community in China were still the White Russians. In August 1938, Lorraine took a holiday in the Japanese-occupied port city of Qingdao (Tsingtao) in Shandong province, famous for its seaside air and brewery and a favourite getaway spot with Shanghailanders. Lorraine stayed in a 'charming villa' kept by the Ignatieff family: the father was a former officer in the Imperial Russian Navy, his wife kept the table supplied with Russian delicacies and their daughter Tania was about Lorraine's age. Also staying in the house were the Chetnikoffs; the father was a former officer in the Imperial Army who had owned a large estate near St Petersburg. After they escaped from the Bolsheviks, Madame Chetnikoff took up dressmaking, and now ran a boutique in Shanghai.

It was the anniversary of the opening of the Battle of Shanghai, and 'trouble'—attacks on the Japanese by Chinese urban guerrillas—were expected in that city. Around Qingdao itself, fighting was going on between the Japanese and the guerrillas, with firing in the hills behind the town, but the main threat facing Lorraine and the young Russian women in the house was being harassed by Japanese soldiers in the streets. Despite this, the Russian emigres placed great store in the Japanese; they sat around fantasising about a hoped-for Japanese invasion of Russia which would overthrow the Soviet regime and restore their lost estates to them. It sounds like the setting of a Chekov play.

Back in Shanghai, Lorraine embarked on another affair, with the Japanese journalist Horiguchi Yoshinori.

Horiguchi had a cosmopolitan background: his father was Japanese and his mother Belgian. Like Edgar Snow he was a graduate of the famed Missouri School of Journalism, and he was married to an American. But his loyalties were with Japan and he combined his job as a correspondent for the official Japanese news agency *Domei* with that of a military spokesman, occasionally donning uniform and carrying sidearms.

Horiguchi was detested by Norman Alley. They got off on the wrong foot during the Battle of Shanghai: in his memoir the American cameraman tells how he had met Horiguchi while he and Philip Stephens were watching the fighting from the balconies of the Cathay Hotel. Alley made a joke about the poor aim of Japanese anti-aircraft gunners, which drew from Horiguchi 'a dirty look that packed more dynamite than any shell that ever hit Shanghai'. Horiguchi also disliked Stephens, who baited him in press conferences, and Alley was convinced that Horiguchi had orchestrated the killing of the British journalist. Then there was what Alley regarded as Horiguchi's hypocrisy in proclaiming 'press internationalism' – the professional solidarity of the journalist's profession – while acting as a spokesman for one of the combatants.

Emily was no indiscriminate hater of Japanese, but she too disliked Horiguchi, describing him as an 'undependable drunk' who 'could be nasty'. And so, when Lorraine began her affair with Horiguchi while his American wife was away, Emily refused to be her enabler. 'I didn't like it and I told her so,' Emily wrote; Lorraine 'understood my point of view; we had no hard words over it, but she didn't want to give up Horiguchi.' And so Lorraine moved out of 1826 Avenue Joffre to pursue her new relationship.

There were more than just personal issues in play. Lorraine's affair with Horiguchi began around the time of the Munich summit meeting, at which Britain and France had tried to appease Hitler by agreeing to his annexation of parts of Czechoslovakia – whatever the strategic and diplomatic arguments in favour, a betrayal of democracy and freedom. Closer to Shanghai, these months also witnessed the battle for Wuhan, the great city in the central Yangtze basin which had become the bastion of Chinese resistance to the Japanese. It was the fall of Wuhan in late October 1938 that prompted the Chinese government to establish its capital in Chongqing, further up the Yangtze.

But if the battlefront was receding into western China, this did not mean that Shanghai was at peace. As the conflict escalated, the foreign enclave became more than ever a strategic prize, and the Japanese and their Chinese collaborators sought to control it through their intelligence apparatus and their allies among the city's criminal gangs. The Chinese *Juntong* fought back, sparking a terrorist war of assassination and counter-assassination, and caught in the middle were the largely British-manned Shanghai Municipal Police, who became the target of attacks by Japanese-backed Chinese gangs. According to Percy Finch, the streets now

> *... became a political battlefield. The bloody welter of Oriental politics, with Chinese Nationalists, Chinese Communists and Japanese ronin in the major roles, and criminal gangs exploiting this anarchy and playing supporting roles, convulsed the city like a sudden plague ... This was a period of armed bodyguards, armor-plated cars, bulletproof vests and street pillboxes ...*

When added to the suffering of the refugees crowded into the foreign settlements, this terrorist conflict meant that the war, rather than having disappeared into the interior of China, was abundantly on show whenever Lorraine went out into the street. And yet she was prepared to break with her best friend to become the mistress of a man who served the cause of all this misery, the Imperial Japanese Army. Why? In Emily's view, it was because Lorraine's time with Tokugawa Iemasa had left her besotted with Japanese influence:

> *I hold no brief for Jean's politics, which are confused. The conquest by Japan of the territory around Shanghai excited and pleased her, and brought back vivid memories of happy old days, quarrelling with her Prince* (Tokugawa). *She was bright enough to realize that her own country and Japan would come to blows sooner or later, but she didn't worry unduly about that. Lingering on the roadside instead of hurrying to cross the bridge, she met Bob Horiguchi, the half-Japanese newspaperman who worked for Domei, and found him attractive.*

Lorraine was not alone in her outlook: at this time, many in the West still supported the soon-to-be enemy countries Germany, Italy and Japan. Many had applauded the Italian victories over the 'barbaric' Ethiopians. Many—particularly Catholics—cheered the Fascists' final victory in Spanish Civil War, which came in February 1939. Many Europeans—and not a few Chinese—supported the Japanese against the Kuomintang. But they wound up on the wrong side of history. Lacking a moral compass and confused by her romantic enthusiasm for Japan, Lorraine held back.

It's at this point that Emily's account of Lorraine in *China to Me* comes to an end; there are no futher mentions of her in the book. And now the two friends took different paths.

The year 1939 was a rough one for Emily, increasingly weighed down by her opium habit and her messy relationship with Shao Xunmei. Nevertheless she embarked on a project which was to occupy her for the next two years: a biography of the Soong sisters—not just the most powerful women, but among the most powerful people, in China.

The eldest was Ai-ling, who was married to the Kuomintang's Finance Minister, then came Ching-ling, the sometime patron of Agnes Smedley and the widow of Sun Yat-sen, the Founding Father of Modern China. The youngest was Mei-ling, the wife of the Kuomintang's leader Chiang Kai-shek. And we recall that their brother, T.V. Soong, had been Lorraine's customer in Louise's brothel.

In June, Emily went to Hong Kong to begin work on the biography, the beginning of a life reset which would see her beat her opium addiction, break up with Shao Xunmei, and move from Shanghai to the new wartime capital Chongqing. As Emily said, 'Shanghai was over for me'. *The Soong Sisters* would be published in 1941.

For her part, Lorraine spent the first seven months of 1939 in

Shanghai before travelling to Australia to reunite her family. We don't know how long her affair with Horiguchi lasted, but her last letter from Shanghai, dated in late July, shows she was still taking a Japanese view of things:

> *Japanese officials I know said that I am going away at a good time as things may become a little nasty ... The corruption of the Chinese Government is appalling ... The rich Chinese here give nothing to help their own soldiers and country, they still spend their money on lavish parties and going to cabarets etc. and then they expect foreign countries to hand out loans ... many people here think that Australia would have no chance in case of attack* (by Japan) *as England would not be able to get assistance through owing to the Japs having their naval bases in many of the Pacific Islands.*

On that chilly and somewhat prescient note Lorraine departed Shanghai. She would never go back, but in another way she never left. Forty years later she would have a large scale, street directory map of 1930s Shanghai hanging on the walls of her London house. From now on, she would belong to the club of former Shanghai inhabitants who, however widely they had dispersed, felt they had been shaped by their time there. And while Lorraine paid a price in shame and regret for her life in the city, that life had also opened vistas to her that she never would have even dreamt of in Australia.

For better and for worse, Shanghai had been the making of her.

Three: The Shady Lady
Sydney 1939–1943

The secret police used what they knew of her
position to recruit her as an informer ...
Rupert Lockwood, *What is in Document J*

I

'Buried alive'

I can't bear the life here

Lorraine Murray to Emily Hahn

Sydney may have been Lorraine's home town, but whenever she was there she was always longing to get away.

She arrived home at the end of September 1939, just weeks after the outbreak of war in Europe, with the firm intention of staying for a few months only. Instead, she wound up marooned in Australia for eight years. And for the first four of these she lived the same sort of life she had in China – although in distinctly less glamorous circumstances. She had affairs, she toyed with regular employment and when money ran short she had recourse to dubious expedients. These years, her early thirties, were the doldrums of Lorraine's life.

The silver lining was her reunion with her family – with her siblings at any rate; relations with her mother Laura could still be problematic. But Lorraine had left behind in China another family of friends and lovers including Edmund, the Italian diplomat Franco Farinacci and above all Emily, and often it seemed that she would never see them again. But the memories of her romantic years in Shanghai never lost their grip on her, and she hungered to relive them.

Sydney was much as Lorraine had left it. The Harbour Bridge had been completed and the AWA tower had become the city's tallest structure, but not much else had changed. Australia had yet to recover from the Depression: Bernard Smith—we recall his experience of growing up illegitimate—recorded in his autobiography that as late as 1939 the streets of Sydney were full of beggars. Even World War II failed to shake things up: for the first few months of the conflict the official watchword was 'business as usual'. The contrast with booming, terrorism-wracked Shanghai could not have been greater.

Within weeks of her arrival home, Lorraine was telling Emily that she was 'fed up with this country'. Australian society was provincial, oafish and repressed; even for those with jobs, money was short and nightlife almost non-existent. She scornfully pointed out that while the Shanghai institution of the 'kept woman' was unheard of, there were 'plenty of girls who just do it for nothing or a few free drinks'. There could be no more damning indication of Sydney's lack of *savoir faire*.

Her mother must have welcomed the prodigal daughter with mixed feelings. Now married herself, Laura's two sons were working in the far west of New South Wales and her youngest daughter Margaret had just married into an established medical family. Living in the genteel North Shore suburb of Killara, Laura must have felt that she had at last succeeded in steering her illegitimate family away from the treacherous shoals of scandal. But now Lorraine had returned from a long and ill-defined sojourn in a city synonymous with vice.

To prepare the ground for her return, Laura had passed some of Lorraine's letters on to the Sydney *Sun*, which had printed extracts from them. These had given an upbeat picture of her life in China as an eyewitness to the Battle of Shanghai, a volunteer nurse's aide, an in-demand society woman and an adventurous tourist. This publicity must have gone some way to answering the inevitable question, 'But what exactly did Lorraine *do* in China?'

Lorraine herself was ready for that question; she had curated a history which threw a cloak of respectability over her time abroad – and Emily was a considerable part of that history. Laura kept a photo of the famous American writer ...

> *'... in the drawing room and she points with pride to it when there are visitors to say that's the Miss Emily who my daughter lived with, then they say what a beautiful face, and Mother adds so pure she looks with so much character, she writes for the New Yorker you know. I don't think any of mother's friends have any idea what the New Yorker is. Anyhow, it somehow justifies my existence in China and eases Mother's conscience ...'.*

But now Lorraine's past started catching up with her. This happened in a minor way when Emily's story 'Russian: Child's Size' appeared in *The New Yorker*. Lorraine started to read the story aloud to a family gathering before realising that the main character, an attention-seeking narcissist nicknamed 'The Girl Who Commits Suicide', was actually a portrait of herself. She passed the episode off as a joke but in the years to come, her appearances in Emily's writings became more and more a source of anxiety.

Prostitution was the elephant in the room. 'I have to be so careful what I talk about,' Lorraine told Emily, recounting an incident involving Hubert Knickerbocker's funny story about Stalin's mother. The punchline, where the old lady asks 'But what is it my son does for a living?', normally sent people into fits of laughter. But when Lorraine told her mother the story, Laura 'broke down and just wept and wept. She said Lorraine you must never tell me those things again ... she had compared herself to Stalin's mother and wondered what her daughter did for a living ...'

Exactly what 'things' had Lorraine been telling her? That she had been Tokugawa's mistress? A sex worker in a Shanghai brothel? A serial 'kept woman'? And why was Laura weeping? Why did her conscience need 'easing'? Was it because she had failed in her maternal duty? Or because she herself had set Lorraine a bad example by living in unmarried sin? There was enough material here to fuel a guilt-and-reproach reaction between mother and daughter for a long, long time, and for decades 'love-hate' would not be too strong a description for their relationship.

They also quarrelled about money:

> *Relations are very strained at home ... mother is angry I think that I have money of my own ... whining and moaning about what she and Charley are going to do when he retires and they will have no money to live on ... I told her she should have thought about that years ago when she was getting one thousand pounds a year income* (a reference to Chaffey's lavish support during the 1920s) ...'

And though Lorraine herself was—thanks to Edmund's largesse—suspiciously flush with cash, she made it clear that there were limits to her contributions to the family finances. She did make a vague offer to help around the house, though she baulked at 'coolie work'—a Shanghailander term meaning the sort of household drudgery best left to servants.

As the weeks went by, Sydney showed no sign of improving.

'I can't bear the life here ... I feel as if I'm buried alive', she wailed to Emily. 'It's the people mainly'. She consoled herself with the thought that she would soon be returning to Shanghai and that, meanwhile, thanks to her allowance, she had enough money to be 'independent and respectable and just amuse myself'. She had rented a flat in Kings Cross to which she could retreat when the joys of family life in Killara began to pall.

As a place to reside in Sydney, Lorraine considered Kings Cross to be the pick of a meagre bunch, and over the next few years she would live in several different flats in and around Macleay Street.

She described the area as 'Bohemian and foreign' on account of its raffish, even cosmopolitan, air—many of the European refugees who had made it as far as Sydney congregated there. The Claremont Café on Darlinghurst Road, for example, was run by the German Walter Magnus, whose willingness to serve alcohol illegally (Australia had a system of partial Prohibition) drew a fashionable clientele including actors like Peter Finch and artists like Donald Friend. And although it would be two decades more before Kings Cross would be able to claim the title of Australia's Capital of Sleaze, the district already had a louche edge to it. The journalist Ronald McKie raved about its

> *... smart metallic women with dubious underclothes and sleek slick males who hunt together and apart, while blonde waitresses, who can be had for a price, shrill orders into the street where lights flicker on dappled trunks of rustling plane trees and ferret-eyed prostitutes saunter under orange signs through polyglot crowds ...*

These few streets were the nearest thing to the Whore of the Orient that Sydney could manage.

Within weeks of her arrival, Lorraine had taken up with a journalist called Bill Rodie, who worked for the jingoistic Sydney newspaper *Smith's Weekly*. Following her affairs in Shanghai, Lorraine clearly now saw journalism as being synonymous with excitement and prestige: Rodie was the third journalist that she had taken as a partner, and there would be at least two more in her future.

To Emily, she reported that Rodie was 'dark and goodlooking with hair like Dee Dee's ... At first I thought perhaps he was Jewish especially as he has been circumcised ...'. Rodie had led a colourful life, knocking around in New Guinea with the young Errol Flynn, and he was a good cook. Moreover, he had read Emily's articles in *The New Yorker*, and so Lorraine could report that she basked 'a little in the glory of having once lived with you'.

So she moved into Rodie's flat in the modernist Wyldefel Gardens apartments in Potts Point. He introduced her to his circle, and at one of these parties she met a group of Italian women. It turned out that she and they had friends in common: the officers from the cruiser the *Raimondo Montecuccoli*, the very same ones who had visited her in hospital in Shanghai after her overdose. The cruiser had subsequently visited Sydney and left a legion of female admirers in its wake. Delighted with these like-minded acquaintances, Lorraine made a date with them to attend a Fascist propaganda lecture at the Italian Consulate.

So life with Rodie had its attractions, but when Lorraine weighed things up these were not enough.

Up until this time, it had been other people who had been advising Lorraine to get married, while she herself had been lukewarm about the idea, preferring, as she said, the freedom of the demimonde. But now, in these early wartime letters to Emily, Lorraine started to talk about potential husbands in a way that shows she had come round to the idea, in theory at least.

One of these potential husbands was William Vero Read, a lawyer from a prominent legal family in Sydney's Eastern Suburbs, whom she described as 'my fiancé'—although 'ex-fiancé' was more accurate. We don't know where and when the two became engaged but whenever it had started, their relationship had now definitely ended and Vero Read didn't take this well: he shirtfronted Rodie, telling him that he had a prior claim on Lorraine. She brushed him off and Vero Read nursed the grudge.

Then there was Rodie himself. He was in the throes of a divorce, and it would be a year before he would be in a position to marry Lorraine—even supposing he and she were minded to. Overall, she judged, their relationship 'doesn't get me anywhere'.

All her life Lorraine was driven by two complementary impulses. One was to conceal shameful aspects of her past; the other, to make it all seem more glamorous. Everyone does this, but she didn't just put a gloss on things, she invented entire episodes to fill the gaps in her life during her long stay abroad. One of these episodes was a journey across Russia on the trans-Siberian railway to Moscow. In the 1930s, many travellers—like Edmund's friend the journalist Edward Ward—had taken this train, and Lorraine would have spoken to people who had made the journey. It was quite the done thing—but there is no record of *her* having done it, and in fact it is impossible to reconcile such a trip with the chronology of her time abroad.

Nevertheless, the visit to Russia became a prominent item in her cv. Two months after arriving back in Sydney she travelled to the mining town of Broken Hill to catch up with her brother Peter. Broken Hill was a hotbed of labour radicalism and on the basis of her trip to Moscow, Peter introduced Lorraine to a group of his fellow miners, socialists from Yugoslavia, as someone who had actually seen the workers' paradise at first hand. She was

> *... the sister who had been to Russia. They asked me many questions about labour conditions ... Hell! I wasn't able to tell them anything so I just quoted from books* (including Edgar Snow's *Red Star over China*) *I'd read and bluffed my way out, as I couldn't very well let down my brother. Then it was suggested that I should speak on Soviet Russia at the Labour Union Meeting, well that was too much. I pleaded out by saying that I would be placed in a compromising and dangerous position and I would be placed on the Gov. black list as having Anti something sentiments ...*

The jokey tone of the letter and phrases like 'bluffed my way out' show that not only had Lorraine not travelled to Soviet Russia, but that Emily knew the story was false.

But this didn't stop Lorraine embroidering the tale further. When she revisited Broken Hill the following August she told the story again, this time to a reporter from the local newspaper, and she added details such as a visit to Lenin's Mausoleum in Red Square. Her epic snow-bound journey across Russia would become imprinted on her family's collective memory: a later version has Lorraine making the journey *after* the outbreak of World War II, as a war correspondent and wearing a military uniform (in the Broken Hill version she is a student.) Decades later she was still telling people that not even the English weather could compare with icy blasts she had braved in Siberia.

Lorraine was now looking forward to her to return to Shanghai. She was getting on splendidly with her younger brother John; he wanted to see the world and they decided to travel to China together. They booked passages but because it was wartime, they needed security clearances to leave Australia. Lorraine gave as her reason for travelling to China that she was planning to marry her 'fiancé' Edmund Toeg—but there's nothing else to suggest that Edmund had in fact changed his mind and was now offering to marry her.

Then, just days before she was due to sail, Lorraine withdrew her application, saying that her plans had changed because Edmund was now coming to Australia. But by this stage the Military Intelligence authorities, who were responsible for issuing security clearances, had grown suspicious of Lorraine and they continued to investigate her anyway.

Their suspicions were fuelled by reports about her Japanese lovers, the eminent statesman Tokugawa Iemasa and the prominent journalist Horiguchi Yoshinori. Then there were the Italians: Luigi Barzini was now reporting from London and Franco Farinacci was acting-Consul General in Shanghai—and *his* father was the 'slavishly pro-German' Roberto Farinacci, a member of the Grand Council of Fascism, which stood at the very apex of Mussolini's regime. Connections like these gave the authorities grounds to believe that Lorraine was, at the very least, favourably disposed towards two potential enemies, Japan and Italy.

Then on 10 May 1940, Germany attacked Western Europe. At a stroke, this broke the spell of 'business as usual' and prompted a surge of enlistment in the armed services. Lorraine's brother John joined the Australian Imperial Force (AIF), but her brother Peter wasn't allowed to enlist because his industry was essential to the war economy. A month later Mussolini declared war on the British Empire, with the result that a swathe of Lorraine's former lovers and current friends officially became enemies.

By now Bill Rodie had moved from the right-wing *Smith's Weekly* to the left-wing *Daily News*. Then in June he too joined the AIF, ending his relationship with Lorraine. The ailing *Daily News* didn't last much longer itself, but for the final months of its existence its editor was the communist journalist Rupert Lockwood—of whom we shall soon hear much, much more. Then on 5th July Lorraine renewed her application to travel to China, and as a result she was called in to an interview with a Lieutenant Reay of Military Intelligence, at which she was categorically refused permission to travel abroad.

The example of Alan Raymond shows that arguably, the authorities were justified in their refusal.

Raymond was the same age as Lorraine and, like her, had grown up on Sydney's North Shore. In 1931 he had drifted north to Asia and in the following years he earned a dubious living, sometimes in Japan, sometimes in Hong Kong but mostly in Shanghai. Noisily anti-British and anti-Semitic, Raymond first came to the notice of the security authorities when he tried to set up a far-right wing group, with members drawn from Australian expatriates in Asia, calling for Australia to sever its political ties with the UK. He was also constantly falling foul of racetrack authorities in Macao, Hong Kong and Shanghai for racefixing.

Raymond had arrived back in Sydney a few months after Lorraine did, and moved into a flat in Potts Point, near where she was living. He worked briefly as a stockbroker's clerk and he and Lorraine may well have rubbed shoulders on the same trams into the city. In May 1940, he published an article in the *Bulletin* magazine arguing that because the Kuomintang regime had lost so much territory to the invading Japanese, it should no longer be recognised as the government of China. This, of course, was the Japanese argument—and one with which Lorraine had, in the recent past, agreed.

But Raymond wasn't prospering and he decided to return to Shanghai. Somehow he passed or avoided the necessary departure security check and in June he went back to China, travelling third-class on a Japanese ship and then vanishing into Shanghai's lower depths. Then, at the outbreak of the Pacific War, the Japanese occupied the International Settlement, bringing down the curtain on the foreign enclave's autonomy. But the advent of Japanese rule gave Raymond his opportunity, and he emerged as the mouthpiece of a Tokyo-sponsored 'Independent Australia League'. This was a propaganda front whose ostensible aim was, in anticipation of Japan's inevitable victory, to obtain better treatment for the Australian population—better treatment, Raymond stressed, than their misguided support for the wicked British imperialists entitled them to. To this end, he made a series of broadcasts commenting on Australian affairs from a pro-Tokyo standpoint. He disappeared after World War II and was never brought to book.

It's unlikely that Lorraine, if she had been allowed to return to Shanghai, would have gone down Raymond's path of outright treason. At heart she was an Empire loyalist, not so much hostile to Britain as she was enamoured of Italians and Japanese. Nevertheless, in the liminal environment of wartime Shanghai, it would have been easy for her to fall into some kind of accommodation with her old Japanese friends. In preventing Lorraine from travelling abroad, the authorities saved her from the temptations of collaboration.

Lorraine spent August and September in Broken Hill, helping

her brother and sister-in-law, who had just had a baby, and when she had returned to Sydney she learnt that Edmund had stopped paying her allowance. We don't know why. If it was a declaration that he wanted to end their strange relationship, it was equivocal because they continued to write to each other.

But now she was definitely on her own, and her money was running out. She had to get a job.

II

'An ordinary wartime informant'

bright, vivacious, intelligent and not of a particularly high moral standard

Desmond Alexander,
Commonwealth Investigation Branch

In November 1940 Lorraine became an informant for the Commonwealth Investigation Branch (CIB), a forerunner of the Australian Security Intelligence Organisation.

Australia was in the throes of a security panic. At the outbreak of the war, there had been a tiny Nazi network operating in the country, which had been quickly rounded up. But then eight months later came the German conquest of Western Europe, which was widely attributed to a largely imaginary 'Fifth Column'. Supposedly, this was a vast conspiracy of traitors whose spying and sabotage had opened the door for the *Wehrmacht*, and it was suspected by analogy that Australia must also be harbouring such an organization, which had hitherto gone undetected. In fact there was no Fifth Column, but this didn't stop the authorities from trying to uncover one.

Previously there had been some categories of people, such as women born in Germany (most German-born men had already been interned) and Jewish refugees from Central Europe, whom the Australian authorities had been content to keep on a fairly loose rein. But now these came under much closer scrutiny, and they were not the only ones. People actually born in Australia but of Italian and German descent also became suspects, as did Anglo-Australians with unorthodox beliefs—like Seventh Day Adventists—or foreign connections. The number of people interned on security grounds jumped and soon the Australian population was under closer surveillance than at any other time prior to the advent of today's national security state.

It was in this climate of fear and suspicion that Lorraine became an informant. She later told the journalist Rupert Lockwood that the CIB had forced her to work for them by threatening to reveal her scarlet past—but it's just as likely she volunteered. Lockwood also noted that Lorraine had been paid by the CIB, and she certainly needed the money. Then again, spying had been part of the thrilling ambience of Shanghai and she may have hoped that working for the CIB might make Sydney more exciting. She had role models: Lockwood would compare Lorraine (unfavourably) to Mata Hari, whose sexy glamour had been imprinted on the public mind by the notorious and wildly successful 1931 biopic starring Greta Garbo.

Lorraine had two qualities which would have made her a good informant: her own sexy glamour, which prompted men to try and impress her, and her fabulist's habit of deceiving people. But she seems to have lacked almost all the other necessary attributes—such as discretion—and at bottom she was ambivalent about the role.

The first record of Lorraine's new occupation is a memo dated 12th November 1940 written by the CIB officer who recruited her, Desmond Alexander. Alexander would later describe her as just 'an ordinary wartime informant'.

Alexander's memo was based on information provided by one of his sources – someone who knew Lorraine – and it is mix of facts, half-truths and errors. It states that she had arrived in Shanghai at the age of ten, having been taken there by a German aunt. She had subsequently travelled in Canada, Russia and Japan and had a working knowledge of Italian, German, Japanese and Chinese. In Shanghai she had worked in the Maskee Bar – described as a 'clearing house for German and Italian agents in the East'. And she had a treasured photo album, which contained numerous photographs of herself with Luigi Barzini and Franco Farinacci. This photo album was indeed Lorraine's great treasure, and it features prominently in her family's memory of her.

According to Alexander's source, Lorraine had now run out of money and options. She had been trying to get a job as a sales assistant, but with no success. Reduced to living with her mother, she was complaining loudly that she was being forced to do 'coolie work' and was so determined to return to Shanghai that she was considering stowing away on a Japanese liner. Based on this hearsay, Alexander had no difficulty in pronouncing judgement on Lorraine: 'This young lady is bright, vivacious, intelligent and not of a particularly high moral standard'.

The inaccuracies in Alexander's memo reflect not only Lorraine's habit of lying about her past, but also the limitations on background checking and surveillance in the pre-electronic age, as well as the particular difficulties the CIB was then facing. Between the wars, the organisation had been focused on two main perceived threats: the Communist Party of Australia and radical labour unionism. It had never been intended to undertake the sort of mass screening of the population required of security intelligence organisations in wartime, and now it had been eclipsed by the much better-resourced Military Intelligence.

Inter-agency rivalry was rife: Military Intelligence had more, and more accurate, information about Lorraine—but then the CIB did not talk to its rivals in the Army. By the time Lorraine went to work for it, the Alexander's organisation was losing the turf battle against its military competitors and soon it would be completely eclipsed.

Despite the CIB's fading star, Alexander was having a productive week. The day before he wrote his memo on Lorraine he had written another, reporting on a conversation he'd had with the journalist and academic Peter Russo, who was almost certainly the source of Alexander's information about Lorraine.

Born in Ballarat, Russo had spent the previous decade in Japan, winding up as a lecturer at the Tokyo University of Commerce. From his Tokyo vantage point, he had become a well-regarded writer on international affairs, contributing articles to the Melbourne *Herald* – owned by Keith Murdoch, founder of the media dynasty. In addition, because of his Italian background, Japanese language skills and wide range of contacts, Russo was occasionally employed as an consultant by the Italian Foreign Ministry. As such, he was well known to Italian diplomats and among the broader Italian community in both Tokyo and Shanghai—a city he frequently visited. These were, of course, the very same circles in which Lorraine was notorious because of her relationships with Barzini, Farinacci and the Italian Legation staff in Beijing. Russo was, and would remain, a valuable source for Alexander into the late 1940s.

The circumstantial case for believing that it was Russo who drew Alexander's attention to Lorraine is strong. Lorraine herself had probably met Russo in Shanghai. Russo routinely acted as a talent spotter for the CIB—he identified other Australians returning home from North Asia who might prove useful as war with Japan loomed. And thirdly, Alexander's memos about

Lorraine and Russo were written within a day of each other, during one of the very few occasions on which they were both in Sydney at the same time.

A few days later, Alexander added an emollient note to the file: 'Saw Miss Murray. She is reconciled to the idea that she should stay in Aust. She proposes purchasing a tobacco kiosk or accepting employment in a coffee lounge'. He was playing down any suggestion that she was a security threat, and the reason for this was that he had recruited her as his informant.

Lorraine's first target was Gerda Holterhoff.

Gerda was born in Sydney in 1912, her parents having arrived from Germany around the turn of the century. They had become naturalised British subjects (that is to say British citizens; a separate Australian nationality did not yet exist) at the outbreak of the First World War. Her father was a partner in a flourishing wool export firm and the family lived in Warrawee, not far from Lorraine's own childhood home. Gerda and Lorraine attended the same school, Abbotsleigh.

After graduating from the University of Sydney with a degree in German, Gerda went to work for the German community newspaper *Die Brucke*. This was financed by the German Consulate in Bridge Street in the city, which also served as the hub of the small Nazi spy ring closed down at the beginning of the war. Gerda had visited Germany on three occasions, most recently in 1936-1937, and on her return she had been employed as a teacher by her old school Abbotsleigh. And then, just hours after World War II had broken out, she had become engaged to Eduard Sieper, a German citizen and the Australian representative of a German firm. Sieper was immediately interned.

The war brought hard times for Gerda and her family. Her

father's business had failed and to support themselves the family had taken over a small retail store in the working class suburb of Glebe. In July 1940, Gerda's 73 year-old father was interned as a threat to national security, but the fact that he was the only one of the family to be detained did not mean that the rest were clear of suspicion—far from it. In September, Gerda had been sacked by Abbotsleigh, effectively for being German; she had gone to work in the family shop in Glebe. And then, just days after Lorraine was recruited by the CIB, she and her mother Laura descended on the Holterhoffs in Glebe. As Gerda recalled:

> *I did not see Lorraine for years and years, and one day her mother rang up and said could she come and see us ... We were amazed, we scarcely remembered her ... We were puzzled that they should seek us out, and they came out, we spent quite a friendly afternoon, she told us of her trip to the East; we told her that my father was interned, and then she told us that because she had been in Japan she had also been questioned a few times at the Intelligence Office.*
>
> *Her mother said she had come out because she had been very lonely since she came back, and she remembered we had been at school together and she thought perhaps we could be friendly. Then we said that one day perhaps she could come out to our place, but she did not come because she was sick and after that we did not take up any connection with her any more, we thought it wiser because she had been questioned at the Intelligence and we did not want to give rise to any suspicion at all.*

Lorraine had been tasked by Alexander to sound out the Holterhoffs' suspected Nazi leanings, but when it came to the point, she couldn't bring herself to violate their trust—so she deliberately blew her own cover by mentioning 'the Intelligence Office'. She went through the motions of informing, but her heart wasn't in it.

This was the end of Lorraine's involvement with the Holterhoffs, but Gerda's subsequent experience illustrates the fate of those who fell foul of Australia's wartime security regime. In July 1941 she herself was interned; she and Sieper were married in the detention camp. Official attitudes towards the two were startlingly vindictive: a 1944 note on her file recommends that her Australian citizenship notwithstanding, at the end of the war Gerda should be deported along with her husband to Germany, on the grounds that she would have become so embittered by her internment as to become a permanent security risk.

In the event, Gerda and her husband were not released until April 1946, and they lived out their lives in Australia.

III

Fighting the Bosses' War

beautiful, irresponsible, vicious and slanderous
Rupert Lockwood, *What is in "Document J"*

In 1939, the Communist Party of Australia (CPA) had only a few thousand members, concentrated on the east coast, particularly around Sydney and its industrial satellites of Newcastle, Lithgow and Port Kembla. But it made up for its small size with a rigorous internal discipline and a clear goal: replacing what the Party saw as Australia's corrupt capitalist government with a socialist state.

Bernard Smith joined the CPA in that year because it offered the hope that 'human affairs could be arranged more rationally and more compassionately than before'. Many others—such as the writer Dymphna Cusack, the chronicler of wartime Sydney—felt the same way. Moscow had become their beacon because, in stark contrast to the Western democracies, the Soviet Union had directly opposed Fascism by supporting the Republican side in the Spanish Civil War. In Bernard Smith's eyes, this made the Soviets the 'only force in the world at time both ready and able to stand up against the might of Hitler and his allies'.

Someone else who joined the CPA in 1939 was Rupert Lockwood,

Lorraine's most prominent target as a CIB informant.

Lockwood began his career as a journalist on Keith Murdoch's Melbourne *Herald*. Leaving Australia in his mid-twenties, he worked in Singapore, passed through Shanghai and then travelled via the Trans-Siberian Railway to London. In June 1937 Lockwood went to Spain, where the Civil War was entering its second year, and stayed for some months filing for the *Herald* from the Republican side. Next year he was back in Australia, working for the *Herald* covering the national Parliament in Canberra. But then Lockwood broke with the Establishment, gave up his job with the *Herald* and moved to Sydney. It was at this point that he joined the CPA but, like Bernard Smith, he kept his membership secret. Lockwood's skills as a writer, publicist and public speaker made him a considerable asset to the Party.

In August 1939, Stalin reversed Soviet foreign policy, signing a pact with the Nazis which turned Russia into a German ally. As a result of this about-turn and following new instructions from Moscow, when war broke out, the CPA, rather than supporting the war against Fascism, denounced the conflict as 'the Bosses' War'. By now, CPA cadres had infiltrated the mining, steel and armaments industries, and the Party mounted an industrial campaign of sabotage against the war effort. In June 1940, the conservative Menzies government proscribed the CPA: the CIB opened a file on Lockwood and Desmond Alexander made it his personal mission to see the charismatic agitator locked up in an internment camp.

Lockwood was now working for the *Daily News*, the failing, left-leaning daily where Lorraine's lover Bill Rodie also worked. When the *Daily News* closed in July, Lockwood kept writing; under his own name for other left-wing publications, and anonymously for the CPA's banned newspaper the *Tribune*, which circulated as an underground publication. But the whole range of the CPA's work had been banned, including holding and speaking at meetings under the party banner, and writing for the *Tribune* was only one of several activities that exposed Lockwood to the risk of internment.

Lockwood's way around the proscription was to use neutral platforms to back policies which advanced the broad aims of the CPA, while avoiding outright statements which could be deemed prejudicial to the war effort. It was a fine line, and Lockwood was good at treading it: he was a brilliant performer at public meetings. One of his arguments was that the Australian authorities were failing to prepare for bombing raids like those which were currently devastating Britain. Even though Pearl Harbour was still more than a year away, Lockwood raised the spectre of Japanese air raids on Sydney and called for the digging of a network of large underground shelters—whose construction would have the additional benefit of employing out-of-work miners. Highly emotive, nominally apolitical, concerned with public safety and alleviating unemployment, Lockwood's campaign for air-raid shelters was hard to argue against.

In the national election of September 1940, standing as an independent but flaunting his communist sympathies, Lockwood won 15% of the vote in a coal mining electorate. He was now a real threat to the war effort, yet he managed to avoid internment—and for this, he would have Lorraine partly to thank.

It was a debt he would only grudgingly acknowledge.

Over the years, Lockwood would refer to Lorraine on three occasions. The first was in a memorandum which, as 'Document J', became a key part of evidence before the Royal Commission on Espionage, set up to inquire into the sensational 1954 defection of the Soviet intelligence officers Vladimir and Evdokia Petrov. In this document, 'Lorraine Murray' is described as a 'very beautiful' but 'remarkably stupid girl' who is set to spy on Lockwood by the sinister and incompetent Desmond Alexander of the CIB.

When the Petrov scandal broke, Lockwood wrote a sanitised version of this original memo, entitled 'What is in "Document J'. Unlike the original it was intended as a public document, and Lockwood was concerned about being sued for libel; as a result Lorraine was not actually named. Nevertheless she was clearly identified as a 'shady lady ... beautiful, irresponsible, vicious and slanderous', who was set to spy on Lockwood by the sinister and incompetent Desmond Alexander.

Then in a 1975 interview with journalist Tim Bowden, Lockwood reminisced about Lorraine, again without naming her. By now, time had worked its healing magic and his memory of Lorraine was kinder.

> *Apparently security had graduated from the slogan of "Reds under the Beds" to "Beds under the Reds"! I had this beautiful girl put on to me (I must say that at least security didn't put any old bag on to me) ... The girl had rather a cosmopolitan background, she was reputed to have been friendly with one of the princely Tokugawas of the old feudal shogunate family in Japan and was well known in the international set in Shanghai and Hong Kong...'*

Lorraine, we know, was a great beauty and Lockwood, according to his contemporary the historian Russel Ward, was a 'fantastically good-looking young man': they must have made a spectacular pair on the drab streets of wartime Sydney. We don't know whether their relationship was a sexual one, but it's pretty clear that Lockwood wouldn't have minded if it had been—and maybe Lorraine felt the same way.

They had first met in early 1940 in the *Daily News* office, where Lorraine used to come in and meet Bill Rodie. After Rodie enlisted in the Army, Lorraine dropped out of Lockwood's sight until he ran across her in the street ...

> *'She claimed she had no ready money and was hungry. From the way she ate the meal I bought her out of pity, this appeared true. But she still retained such trinkets from the past as a sable coat. The lady had been in the hands of the Commonwealth Investigation or Security Police, who were well aware of her character. The secret police used what they knew of her position to recruit her as an informer ...'*

This was in Kings Cross. Soon after going to work for the CIB, Lorraine had moved into a flat on Elizabeth Bay Road, which would become her home for the next two years. It was a crowded precinct: Alexander and Lockwood, hunter and quarry, were both living nearby on Macleay Street and Dymphna Cusack was a bit further away, soaking up the impressions of street life that she would use to such good effect in the novel *Come In Spinner*, her panorama of the wartime city.

Then one day in May 1941, Lorraine was in Potts Point post office when she bumped into her old acquaintance Barbara Davies, whose fashion triumph at a Royal garden party in London four years earlier had excited Lorraine's envy. Davies lived nearby and invited Lorraine home for lunch, but they failed to bond because, in Davies' words, Lorraine did not seem like 'a very honest or trustworthy person'. Over lunch, Davies—a civilian employee of the Royal Australian Navy—had unwisely boasted that she was a good friend of Lockwood's and Lorraine, with more than a hint of schadenfreude, passed this snippet on to Alexander.

Here was Lockwood apparently cultivating a Navy employee with access to classified material; Alexander seized on Lorraine's tipoff and a few days later he confronted Davies, threatening her over her connection with the communist subversive. But his intervention backfired badly, because Davies actually worked for one of the CIB's military rivals, the Naval Intelligence Division—a much bigger bureaucratic beast than his own organisation. Alexander was forced to retract his comments and his boss was compelled to apologise. A humiliation for the CIB, the incident suggests that Alexander and Lorraine were something of a dysfunctional duo, an impression confirmed by what happened next.

The conservative Menzies government lacked a majority in parliament, so it had to tread carefully to avoid antagonizing the Left. And Lockwood had considerable standing among the labour movement: he was no Gerda Holterhoff, an unknown young woman who could be slung into detention without worrying about public reaction. So in order to get him interned, the CIB had to do it by the book, to produce hard evidence of Lockwood actually undermining the war effort—such as directly calling on men not to enlist in the armed services. But this was difficult to obtain: according to an irritated note on his file, Lockwood's 'veiled references to the Prime Minister, the Federal Government and the war effort brand him as a disloyal defeatist'—and the word 'veiled' was the nub of the problem. He was skirting around the letter of the proscriptions.

By now, Lorraine was well placed to help Alexander get that evidence. According to her file, she and Lockwood were 'on a very friendly basis ... she attends the street corner meetings to hear him speak'. And so when Lockwood told Lorraine he was due to address a meeting in Kings Cross, she set him up. She informed Alexander, who commandeered a flat next to the spot where the communist was due to speak. Concealed in the flat he installed a shorthand note taker who would take down Lockwood's exact words. According to Lockwood ...

> *Alexander stupidly bargained that, if I thought there were no shorthand writers present, I would not be as careful as usual in phrasing my speech, and that I might make ... a "subversive" statement against the Government's policies, to provide a pretext for internment.*

The trap was set. But then Lorraine, just as she had in her dealings with Gerda Holterhoff, let her feelings override other considerations, and

> *now apparently more fond of me than she was of the political police and having a heart of somewhat tarnished gold,* (she) *warned me that Mr Alexander had said that he had had enough of my seditious oratory and would "get me" ... Having been warned by Alexander's irresponsible lady informer of the plan, I kept close watch on the darkened windows. Sure enough, I noted the flutter of white paper as the pages of short-hand notebooks were turned over.*
>
> *Suddenly and melodramatically I drew the attention of the crowd to the shorthand writer hidden in the half gloom and began to shout indignantly about the Gestapo invading Australia, about contemptible spying on Australian democrats, about the menaces of secret police pimping and so on ... Alexander who was at the meeting left very hastily.*

The crowd by this time was quite angry …

Soon after this incident the Germans launched their invasion of the Soviet Union and the CPA changed its policy again, switching from obstructing the war effort to mobilizing maximum support for it. With the Soviets now fighting alongside the Allies, Canberra eventually lifted the ban on the CPA and Lockwood emerged openly as Assistant Editor of the *Tribune*.

Lorraine's role in Alexander's attempt to entrap Lockwood might seem like a bit-part in a farce—but the CPA wasn't a joke. The communists were in deadly earnest, and when Soviet intelligence began its operations in Australia in 1943 the Party had a cadre of committed and well-placed activists—Lockwood among them—standing ready to assist Moscow Centre. Over the following decade, Soviet spying in Australia would have a considerable impact, both on the country's domestic politics and, crucially, on its foreign and national security policy.

IV

Reform

Don't be angry with me, Mickey
Lorraine Murray to Emily Hahn

As Lorraine followed Lockwood around the streets of East Sydney, she herself was being stalked—by the fear that the strongest bond to her golden, romantic life in China was broken. Because in mid-1940 Emily, then living in the Chinese capital of Chongqing, had written the 'flibbertigibbet' a scorching letter, criticising her for parasitism, for wasting her life, and for lacking a moral compass. She concluded by breaking off their friendship.

Since parting in Shanghai the year before the two women had been on diverging paths. Lorraine—and this would be her own judgement—had remained the same narcissistic, bitchy butterfly she had been: she was still Jean. But Emily was no longer the indulgent agony aunt of 1826 Avenue Joffre. Leaving behind her opium habit and her relationship with Shao Xunmei, she had thrown herself into writing the biography of the Soong sisters. Her previous work, she said, 'had been make-believe', now she was 'carving out a career'. Living in Chongqing, where the Soongs were based, she was drawn into the very vortex of the war. She had dived 'into China, into the war and into real life'.

This was no exaggeration. By April 1940 Chongqing had

become the most heavily bombed city in the world, as the Japanese launched repeated air raids to try and break the resistance of the Chinese. Then in May came the news of the German conquest of Western Europe, which electrified the city's foreign community. Emily became immersed in the catastrophe of the fall of France and the drama of Dunkirk, and watched as British friends raced home to defend their country. With cities in flames, people dying in droves around her, and her friends going off to fight for democracy, Emily lost patience with Lorraine's whining about the lack of a night life in Sydney.

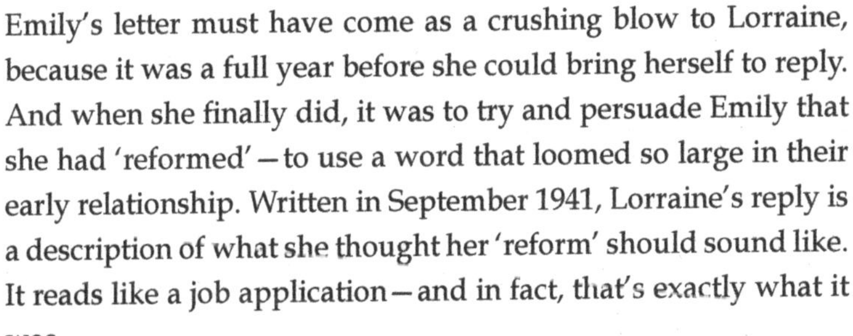

Emily's letter must have come as a crushing blow to Lorraine, because it was a full year before she could bring herself to reply. And when she finally did, it was to try and persuade Emily that she had 'reformed'—to use a word that loomed so large in their early relationship. Written in September 1941, Lorraine's reply is a description of what she thought her 'reform' should sound like. It reads like a job application—and in fact, that's exactly what it was.

The letter starts with an account of her visit to Broken Hill to help her brother and sister-in-law with their new baby. She had, she said, taken the opportunity to go back and 'start right at the bottom and get a new set of values'. 'Rising at dawn and working hard in rather primitive conditions and breathing the pure desert air ... returning to Sydney I felt strong and a new being.'

Thus reborn, Lorraine received the news that Edmund had stopped paying her allowance with equanimity. Rather than being a blow, his decision chimed with her new-found determination to support herself, and turned out to be 'the best thing that ever happened' to her. It prompted her to take a job working in a factory that made ammunition boxes, where she shared the lot of ordinary humanity:

> *The girls and men were such a decent lot and there was good comradeship and lots of fun ... it was funny to think of Wunsy, Johnny Jean of Connaught Road and the Maskee and places East receiving a factory pay envelope for hard work ... yes it was coolie work too ...*

This strikes an uplifting chord—but there is no evidence that Lorraine ever worked in a factory. We do know that during this period she was an informant for the CIB, and their files don't record her as having such a job. And she didn't mention it when she was later being interviewed by the authorities for a security clearance—despite the fact that it would have stood to her credit. So the ammunition box factory sounds like the trip to Moscow, one of those stories which conveniently accounted for periods in Lorraine's life she wanted to gloss over.

After the factory, Lorraine continued, she had worked as a nanny for a Viennese refugee couple—and this job *is* corroborated in the CIB files. Then she had gone back to business college for yet another stint at improving her stenographic and typing skills, and at the time of writing her penitential letter to Emily she was, she said, working as a typist in a lawyer's office.

But donning the hair shirt of regular employment was only one aspect of Lorraine's reform, the external, or social. There was also an internal, a spiritual, aspect to it. Lorraine tells Emily how she had attained humility, purging herself not just of idleness and parasitism, but vanity itself: 'I know I don't look very attractive now, I'm eight pounds heavier in weight feel dull in the brain, not wanting to attract the opposite sex ... Don't care if I have new clothes which is just as well ...'

And she swears that she has left the demimonde: 'I'd never go back to the old existence again ...'

The message was clear: she had mended her ways. And yet in one way she hadn't changed at all: just as she had a decade before, she now badly wanted to get out of Australia. Having done her penance in the desert and on the factory floor, she was now craving readmittance to the paradise of expat life in China – and she begged Emily to get her a job there. If Emily could rustle up even just an offer of employment, this might persuade the Australian authorities to allow her to travel back to China:

> '*Wouldn't I have a lot of face* (meaning prestige or respect) *if I got to H'kong or Sh'hai and got an office job there, just think of it. I'll have references too to show them. Mickey if you hear of anything and you wrote to me about a letter I could show the authorities perhaps I'd be able to go ... Mickey darling, if you have time write me a tiny tiny little note. Don't be angry with me cos of past happenings ... And if you think I could get an office job please tell me.*

We don't know whether Emily replied to this letter; maybe not, because she had a lot of other things on her mind. In late 1940, having finished her research in Chongqing, she had moved to Hong Kong where she renewed her acquaintance with Charles Boxer, the British military intelligence officer who had called on her in Shanghai. Emily and Boxer began a relationship and she gave birth to their daughter Carola in October 1941.

And so Emily and baby Carola were in Hong Kong when it was overrun by the Japanese two months later. Boxer, who was wounded in the battle, became a prisoner of war. Most European, American and Australian women in Hong Kong were interned, but Emily managed to avoid this because the Japanophile Boxer had good contacts among the invading army. When the occupiers came to know of Emily's relationship with Boxer, they were disposed in her favour and she was left at semi-liberty, though unable to leave Hong Kong.

But contact between Emily and Lorraine was severed, and it would be three years before it would resume.

V

'A LOT OF GOOD LAUGHS'

Baby, don't you know that it's rude
To keep my two lips waiting when they're in the mood
Andy Razaf, *In the Mood*

LORRAINE AND Lockwood had become entangled during some of the darkest days of the war. While she had been sabotaging the authorities' attempts to throw the Communist Party's star agitator into detention, the Germans had been conquering Greece, capturing five thousand Australian soldiers in the process. Then in July 1941, Japanese forces surged into southern Indochina and Washington responded by imposing economic sanctions against Tokyo, the move which would trigger the attack on Pearl Harbour. And when the Pacific War did break out in December, it became the turning point in Australia's modern history: the moment at which the United States began to replace Britain—strategically, politically and, increasingly, culturally—as the country's dominant external influence. Lorraine would be an interested observer of that transition.

Sydney's reaction to the outbreak of the Pacific War and the subsequent Fall of Singapore was blind panic: for much of 1942, the population lived in real fear of a Japanese invasion. There was a race to put the city in a state of defence: street and household lighting was shrouded—the 'brownout'—and ocean beaches were festooned with barbed wire. The bulk of the AIF, the most effective part of the Army, was in the Middle East, and those troops left available to defend the country were ill-prepared. As Lorraine later told Emily: 'We were very jittery'.

And then American troops started arriving, turning Australia into their main base for the war in the South Pacific.

'War aphrodisia' is a term for the oft-observed phenomenon of a sharp rise in sexual activity in wartime. The effects of conflict—lengthy separations, tedious wartime jobs, a thriving black market, sudden economic opportunity, a dearth of familiar partners contrasted with an influx of exotic strangers, not to mention a fear of sudden death—all these conspire to loosen restraint. (The artist Lucien Freud—admittedly an outlier—said of wartime London 'You couldn't go out in the blackout without getting the clap'.) And when the Americans started flooding into Australia, the effect on the inhabitants was electrifying. As historian Max Hastings put it, they embraced the Americans, and in the case of Australian women, 'this was not merely figurative'.

In her novel *Come In Spinner,* Dymphna Cusack described the American invasion as 'a wave that bore on its crest orchids, nylons, exquisite courtesy, Hollywood lovemaking and a standard of luxury that had never before penetrated below the privileged ranks of the socialites'. Lightning romances and brief encounters erupted, as did casual prostitution, with 'good-time girls' flocking to supply the booming wartime demand for sex. High heels became known as 'Yank-snatchers'.

Kings Cross revelled in the influx. One of the characters in *Come In Spinner,* the ingénue Monnie—who, like Miss Jill, would be trafficked into prostitution—was entranced by the scene on Darlinghurst Road:

> *She wondered what so many people were doing out so late at night ... Men lolled in doorways and against shop windows, ogling the parading girls ... Girls stopped to talk with them; couples went by, arms entwined, staring into each other's eyes, and there were snatches of strange conversations and the chatter of unfamiliar tongues ... How she envied the girls, all so pretty, so smart, so gay. What splendid, well-paid jobs they must have.*

The soundtrack to this amorous American invasion was the Glenn Miller Band's version of 'In the Mood'—in mid-1942 was the most popular tune in Australia. And to Lorraine the excitement, the fleeting opportunities and the flurry of arrivals and departures came as a tonic. She later said of this time, 'I certainly had a good time & lots of fun, though I did work at odd times, believe it or not'. Sydney wasn't dull anymore and one reason was that people whom she had known in China started turning up there, briefly reviving the romance of her life in Shanghai.

In March 1942 General Douglas MacArthur established his General Headquarters in Australia. This became the main source of news for the South West Pacific Theatre, and so it attracted a flock of American journalists, among them Hubert Knickerbocker and Norman Alley. Alley would stay in Australia for more than a year, keeping a flat in Sydney's Eastern Suburbs as his base and maintaining it, he said, 'like an American club'—keeping open house for his compatriots.

Along with orchids and stockings the Americans brought employment opportunities, and Lorraine soon got a job with the United States Army Forces in Australia, USAFIA, an administrative and supply organisation. In her application she gave her age as 26 (it was actually 32) and as references she said that she had worked for one year as a typist for Emily Hahn and for three months as a typist for Hubert Knickerbocker—considerable exaggerations, but who does not burnish their cv? When her American interviewer asked how they could contact Emily in order to check her reference, Lorraine's reply was bulletproof: they couldn't, because she was a Japanese prisoner in Hong Kong.

Lorraine's first stint as 'an employee of Uncle Sam' lasted for eight months. She worked in the Grace Building, the skyscraper-gothic building on York Street, which had been taken over by the American military authorities. According to what she later told Emily, Lorraine started off in the typing pool, then graduated to the position of file clerk in G-2, the generic term for the intelligence staff of a US Army unit.

Lorraine also required a separate security check, which she somehow passed despite Australian Military Intelligence's poor opinion of her. For this security check she gave as a referee the name of Harold Timperley, the Australian journalist who had been the correspondent for the *Manchester Guardian* during the Battle of Shanghai. The war had brought Timperley to Sydney and now, according to the file, he had a 'very high opinion' of Lorraine.

For someone born in the 19th century Harold Timperley had what strikes as a very modern career. Starting off as a journalist and China expert, he went on to become a humanitarian activist, political lobbyist and spook before winding up as an international civil servant and consultant. He had the careerist's gift of conjuring organisations to do his bidding, moving constantly, effortlessly, always upwards. He also had a taste for younger women.

During the Battle of Shanghai, Timperley had combined writing for the *Manchester Guardian* with promoting the Chinese government's public relations campaign, and he was among the first journalists to report on the Rape of Nanjing. By 1939 he was working full time for the Chinese Ministry of Information with the title 'Adviser to the Chinese Government', in a role that went well beyond just public relations to include lobbying and confidential diplomacy.

Lorraine and Timperley may already have crossed paths in Shanghai, but she first met him for certain in late 1941, while he was in Sydney on a speaking tour on behalf of the Chinese government. Timperley then went on to the United States but returned in early 1942, and this time he would stay in Australia for a year. During this time he and Lorraine began a relationship, one which he at least took seriously.

Timperley was a networker before the term existed. Though much younger than Prime Minister John Curtin, they had been journalists together in Perth in the early 1920s and when he visited Canberra he dropped into Curtin's office for a chat. Timperley spent most of his time moving between Sydney and Melbourne, giving talks in support of China and writing propaganda articles with titles like: 'Would you like to spend your next Christmas as a Japanese prisoner?' Then in August, just as he and Lorraine were starting to spend more time together, he joined the Far Eastern Liaison Office, a military intelligence organisation which conducted information or 'political' warfare against the Japanese. He stayed on the Chinese payroll as well.

Lorraine, who dubbed their relationship 'the T episode', was ambivalent about Timperley. She would later describe him to Emily as a man who, for all his professional success, seemed strangely remote and insecure:

> *I found T. very hard to take and after getting to know him better thought there was something "phony" about him, but felt sorry for him ... such a lost lonely soul. When he had his suite of rooms at the Hotel Australia he complained about the lack of good food, the lack of service ... when I suggested he should throw a cocktail party, he told me he hated people round him. He really is a perfect example of an introvert. Also he spent most of his spare time at a psychiatrist here who charged him "through the nose". I suggested he talk to me as he would the psychiatrist, and save his money.*

At some point Timperley proposed to Lorraine, but she turned him down and by April 1943 he had gone back to the United States for good. At the time she didn't seem to miss him much but after the war was over she regretted having let him slip through her fingers on purely practical grounds: as a husband living in America, he would have been her ticket out of Australia.

One of the reasons Lorraine had rejected Timperley's proposal was that she was having more fun with Norman Alley of whom she said 'he had a marvellous sense of humour ... we had a lot of good laughs'. Alley was not only more human, but he could be useful, too; he was, for example, on good terms with William MacKay, the flamboyant Commissioner of the New South Wales Police. When Lorraine's Elizabeth Bay Road flat was burgled and some of her prized mementoes of her time in Shanghai—'the hallmarks of my Far Eastern success'—were stolen, Alley enlisted McKay's personal support and some of her trophies recovered.

While Lorraine was wavering between Timperley and Alley, the Australian government set its face against the kind of pleasures which made the company of these well-paid journalists so enjoyable.

In October 1942, with the Japanese threat to Australia at its height, Prime Minister Curtin launched an Austerity Campaign to curb frivolity and unnecessary consumption. As Curtin told the nation: 'Every day you read about some man you knew dying fighting far distant from the places of entertainment, of even relaxation … Let us think about them a little more and think about ourselves a little less.'

And Lorraine *was* actually thinking about a far-away soldier: her brother John, currently embroiled in the El Alamein campaign in Egypt, in which his 9th Division lost over six hundred dead. This, at least, is what she would tell Emily later:

> *Timperley wanted me to go away some place for a weeks' holiday with him. That was quite out of the question ... I was enthusiastically patriotic and Churchill's speeches were plastered around my room, so I wouldn't think of playing Hookey from work.*

But soon after refusing Timperley's offer of a 'holiday' because she was working too hard, Lorraine was sacked—for not working hard enough.

Her file says that Lorraine was dismissed because she had been 'most unreliable and inefficient'; that she had been 'found to be unsatisfactory'. Later, she would tell Emily a different story: that she had been sacked because her scarlet past had caught up with her. In this version, her supervisor had decided to check her record and 'my dossier was brought to him with the Tokugawa period in black & white … someone certainly kept track of my doings those years in China ... I had to leave Int. G-2 section for good'. As an explanation for being sacked, it sounds much better than being 'unreliable and inefficient'.

Whatever the reason for her sacking, Military Intelligence was still keeping its eye on Lorraine. A few weeks later a report appeared on her file to say that since losing her job, Lorraine had been being supported by Norman Alley. To this report a note was added by Captain Reay—the same officer who had interviewed her three years before. Reay now commented:

> *I remember interviewing Miss Murray in connection with her passport application to proceed to the Far East. She impressed me as a person who might do anything for good cash. She made no bones about having lived with Tokugawa an ex Consul General for Japan. Do not consider her to be anti-British but could be easily led to assist any nationality provided the money was right.*

Without a job, Lorraine was in a vulnerable position; there were various ways in which the authorities could make her life unpleasant. Wartime employment was managed by a system of civilian conscription called 'manpower regulation', which could force her into one of the many boring and dirty jobs essential to the war effort. A well-known hazard of wartime life, there was a slang term for it: to be 'manpowered' meant to be forced into a tedious and badly paid job. There was even a danger Lorraine might wind up in a real ammunition box factory.

And the black marks on her security file kept accumulating. In May 1943, Military Intelligence received another report from an informant about an 'attractive girl' named Lorraine Murray. According to this very garbled report, she had been living abroad with a Japanese nobleman, but when he discovered her in a compromising position with a wealthy Italian, he had cast her off and sent her back to Australia. The really damning part of the report was that she spoke excellent Japanese.

In fact, the informant's source was Lorraine's disgruntled ex-fiancé William Vero Read, and the report summed up Lorraine's image as seen through the bottom of a beer glass: alluring, dangerously intelligent and irredeemably defiled by sexual liaisons with Japanese and Italians.

It was time for a new town, and a new leaf. She wheedled her way into a new job with the American Army, and moved north to Brisbane.

Four: Miss Jill
Brisbane 1943 – London 1948

... start right at the bottom and get a new set of values
Lorraine Murray to Emily Hahn

I

'An honest working girl'

I enjoy my role of respectability & am more or less a useful member of the community ...

Lorraine Murray to Emily Hahn

Of all Australian cities, Brisbane was the most affected by World War II. During its course over two million service and civilian personnel passed through the city: mainly Americans but British, Dutch, Indonesians, Canadians and Chinese as well as men and women from all over Australia. When Lorraine arrived in mid-1943, there were over seventy thousand Americans in and around the city, about one for every five Australians – ten times the ratio in Sydney. Twenty five thousand Australian civilians, many of them women, were employed in clerical, administrative and labouring jobs in support of the Allied military.

Quiet, provincial Brisbane had never seen anything like it. Wartime aphrodisia was rampant, the black market ubiquitous, opium and amphetamines freely available. Prostitutes and criminals flocked to the city. There was an explosion of Chinese restaurants, jitterbug competitions shook the dancehalls, and illegal gambling rooms popped up everywhere. The artist Donald Friend, terminally disenchanted with Army life, had been posted to a disciplinary labouring unit in Brisbane as punishment for continually going absent without leave. Friend, who was gay, described his experience in the city as being one of 'too much drink and sex and general promiscuity'. This was not the outcome his infuriated commanding officer had looked for, but it bears out that for a while, Brisbane was the liveliest place in Australia.

The party began in mid-1942, when General MacArthur had moved his General Headquarters to Brisbane, taking over the top floor of the AMP Building on Edward Street. For living accommodation he and his senior aides moved into Lennon's, Brisbane's newest hotel. The Americans requisitioned buildings and vacant land all over the city: Victoria Park, on the city's northern outskirts, became the site of Camp Victoria, an administrative and accommodation complex occupied by the United States Army Services of Supply (USASOS). This was the logistics organisation responsible for the infrastructure that paved the way to the Allied victory in the South West Pacific Area and Lorraine would live in Camp Victoria, working for USASOS, for about a year.

Now having moved away from Sydney, Lorraine resumed writing letters to her mother Laura, and one of these explains how she managed to get hired by the Americans in Brisbane despite having been sacked by them in Sydney. She identifies the officer who had used his influence to get her a new job, and who was now her boss in USASOS: his name was Lieutenant Colonel Douglas Mapes, and it seems he was besotted with her. But throughout their non-relationship Lorraine played him perfectly; as she would later boast to Emily: 'To tell you the truth, Mapes was one of my Promotion through "Friendship" victims'. It was a victory for the 'little stenographess'.

Lorraine had to negotiate with Mapes to get and to keep her job. When he saw Lorraine's security file detailing her relationships with prominent Japanese and Italians, he like others considered that these made her a security risk. As she later explained to Emily, Lorraine resorted to telling the truth: 'In desperation I told Mapes that I'd been "kept by men" & everything I'd done had been for economic reasons ... So we became friends'. But she was also, she told Emily, careful to keep her relationship with the married colonel on the right side of propriety: 'I was an Honest working girl & never heard him say I'll give you a present. Got the raise in salary which was on Uncle Sam & never cost that guy a penny ...'

With Laura, Lorraine was more circumspect. 'I've had to handle the colonel situation very tactfully,' she wrote:

> *I let him take me to dinner at Lennons the other evening and he told me he is infatuated with me and will be getting a divorce so wants to marry me, and every time he steps into this office about some business, he gets a goofy look on his face and acts silly. Anyhow I'm quite master of the situation, and Brisbane is a very safe place to be in as hardly anyone, no matter how high ranking, except the generals have billets of their own and the Col. is in a hotel, and a very strict rule is that no women are allowed in their places at all, and everywhere you go you are in crowded areas and under the eyes of military police ...* (nevertheless it is) *uncomfortable to go down town the streets are thronged with soldiers and sailors of all forces on leave ...*

In fact, the habit of senior American officers keeping Australian concubines was one of the scandals of the day, the most flagrant example being set by MacArthur's Chief of Staff General Richard Sutherland. His mistress was the socialite Elaine Clark, whose soldier husband was serving overseas. Sutherland installed

Clark as a receptionist at MacArthur's office and then later, when General Headquarters moved north to the war zone, he made her an officer in the US Army's Women's Army Corps and took her with him.

Lorraine would recall how the American top brass—she mentions Generals Kenney, Krueger, Chamberlin and Donaldson as well as Admiral Halsey, naval commander of the South Pacific Area—were frequently to be seen in Brisbane with 'fluffy blondes'. Most of these, she judged, were so common that Madam Louise would never have employed them in her brothel. They ranged from moneyed socialites to working class belles, and Lorraine remarked on how their American paramours were oblivious to the differences in social rank which were so keenly felt by the women themselves—a theme that Dymphna Cusack played up in *Come In Spinner*. As Lorraine said:

> *At some parties, the socialites used to feel very insulted & one general had a milk bar girl as the girl friend – I used to be very amused at the snobbishness on the part of the girls & the man not giving a dam about it ...*

Like all Australians, Lorraine was astonished at the resources that the Americans could conjure up. The staff accommodation in Camp Victoria was criticised for its lavishness by Australian inspectors who were shocked to find the temporary facility had hot water and sewerage systems, paved roads and lawns—all quite at odds with the spirit of Prime Minister Curtin's Austerity Campaign. Lorraine found Camp Victoria 'more comfortable than any other place I've lived in Sydney ... being by myself in the office and (*with*) a lovely view from the window, is quite something'.

She had fallen on her feet.

She described her daily round to Laura. 'We work six full days a week. After breakfast I get to the office about 8 am, dust and tidy up the desks, an hour break at lunchtime, and then working until 5:30, once a week we have a rest day. For Australian girls we are paid considerably well ...'. Wartime workplaces such as USASOS brought women together, sparking bonds of companionship some of which lasted for decades, and it's from this point in her correspondence that we start to hear more about Lorraine's female friends. She had found her tribe.

Soon she was having the most fun she'd had in years.

> *I'm getting too many invitations ... Last night I was invited to Lennon's hotel dinner dance. This is a regular Friday night specialty and they limit the number through bookings, have a good American orchestra too and a lovely floor ... My partner was Captain Jo. Henderson, a very popular and charming fellow ...*

All and all, Lorraine felt that her life in Brisbane was 'reminding me very much of China'—and there could be no higher praise than that. One of the reminders was the Hollywood star Phyllis Brooks, who arrived in Brisbane to entertain the American troops. Brooks had recently appeared on Australian cinema screens in Joseph von Sternberg's *The Shanghai Gesture*, playing the demimondaine Dixie Pomeroy.

The tagline for the movie was 'Shanghai—Where Women are Weak!'.

And now Emily resurfaced. She and her daughter Carola were repatriated from Hong Kong to the United States in September 1943, as part of an exchange of civilians between the Japanese and the Allies.

Lorraine's first letter to the liberated Emily contained no hint of their previous quarrel, but rather, it picked up where her last letter left off: she has reformed.

> *I don't know how I could ever have lived like I did when you knew me. I enjoy working and my independence so much ... I feel confident I could hold down any stenographic job after the experience I have gained here ...*

But she still wants to get out of Australia. Badly.

> *I just couldn't live in this country Mickey after the war, it has always seemed so dead to me and outlook so insular ... so behind in things ... it has taken a Yank invasion to shake them up. I would like to return* (to Shanghai) *but it will be a very different China after this war ends and doubt if we foreigners will be welcome ...*

Now there was a new element in their conversation: marriage had become more urgent. 'At my age it is difficult to meet men who are not already married.' And so Emily's mentorship expanded to take on the role of matchmaker as well, and the question of a suitable husband for Lorraine starts to crop up frequently in their letters.

From Brisbane, Lorraine passed on news of old Shanghai friends—like Walter Fuchs, the German diplomat who had been persecuted by the Nazis, and was currently interned in Shanghai. She had received a postcard from him, but this had proved 'a bit embarrassing'. Because Shanghai was under Japanese occupation, Fuchs' postcard should have come through the hands of the neutral Red Cross. Somehow it didn't, and as a result Lorraine had once more to explain herself to the security authorities.

Fuchs' postcard was a niggling example of how, ever since Lorraine's return to Australia, her past had kept on turning up like a bad penny. It had complicated relations with her family, made her an object of suspicion to officialdom and made it harder for her to get and keep a job. And now it ambushed her again, this time in the form of a woman called Dodie Beatty who was working for the Australian Red Cross in Brisbane. Dodie was the ex-wife of Bill, the boyfriend of Madam Louise, and while she herself was unaware that Lorraine had ever worked in a brothel or had known Bill, the connection was still too close for comfort. It was a very small world.

Over the next few years, Lorraine and Dodie would become friends, but their friendship was a fraught one. On the one hand, Dodie was a reminder of Lorraine's golden age of romance and excitement, and she would prove a loyal ally who networked on Lorraine's behalf. On the other, to Lorraine she embodied the threat of being exposed as a former prostitute. It's a testament to Lorraine's skill at curating her past—a skill inherited from Laura—that she would keep up their relationship for several years without Dodie ever suspecting that her new bestie had met her ex-husband in his girlfriend's whore house.

In September 1944, MacArthur's General Headquarters moved from Brisbane north to the war zone and USASOS headquarters went with it, bringing to an end Lorraine's most fulfilling experience of employment so far. The US Army had been deploying increasing numbers of its Women's Army Corps (WAC) overseas and, in preparation for the move north, American WACs had taken over the jobs of the Australians working in USASOS headquarters. (At this time Australian women—with the exception of nurses—were not allowed to serve in actual combat zones.) Colonel Mapes replaced Lorraine with a WAC—a 'luscious' one, she noted sourly—but he softened the blow by giving her fulsome references. Nor did he forget her.

Lorraine at first considered joining the Australian Women's Army Service—the Australian equivalent of the American WAC. But in the event, she stayed with the Americans and her first move was to a clerical position in another organisation, United States Army Forces in the Far East, which handled staff administration. She didn't enjoy this much but then she was moved to an even less congenial job in a US Army canteen, 'hash-slinging (i.e. serving mashed potato) ... with a lot of Bomb-Happy GIs—psycho cases waiting transportation home'. (Like the public conversation about suicide, discussion of PTSD was a lot less sensitive then than it is today.) And then, after a few months in the canteen, she escaped back to secretarial work with a different employer.

Following the Japanese conquest of the Netherlands East Indies, the Dutch government had set up an administration in exile in Australia to prepare for the recovery of their lost colonial empire. At the end of 1944, Lorraine went to work for this NEI administration, which was based in Camp Columbia at Wacol to the southwest of Brisbane, now engulfed by suburbia but then, as she put it, 'miles out of the city'. Dodie Beatty was also working there, and it sounds like she had got Lorraine the job.

Wacol had its drawbacks: cut off from the sea breezes, it was stifling. Worse, the Dutchmen in the Wacol Camp proved poor substitutes for the departed Americans. 'I miss all the G.I. wolves', Lorraine told Emily, 'here we are just ignored'—but to compensate, Wacol had 'a Far East atmosphere ... with Malays (*Indonesians*) acting as servants ...' Then after three months in

Camp Columbia, Lorraine shifted to a new job as welfare officer for NEI staff in a hostel in Bulimba, south across the river from central Brisbane. This brought more responsibility and better still, she made a friendship which would last the rest of her life, with a woman named Hazel Jones.

Hazel held a highly classified position in the Allied Intelligence Bureau (AIB), the umbrella organisation overseeing intelligence collection and special operations in the South West Pacific Theatre. Lorraine found her 'sympathetic' and decades later she would recall how during the humid Brisbane nights 'Hazel & I would sit on the hostel steps to get fresh air & talk & make plans for the future ...'.

As well as making new friends, Lorraine wondered about old ones. When Mussolini's regime collapsed at the end of April 1945, there was a reckoning for its adherents and the Fascist grandee Roberto Farinacci, the father of Lorraine's close friend Franco Farinacci, was executed by Italian partisans. To Emily, Lorraine mused about the fate of the Italians they had known in Shanghai: 'Wonder what has happened to little Franco & Luigi & the rest of the crowd?'.

As it happened, 'little Franco & Luigi' had both successfully navigated Mussolini's fall from power. Choosing to oppose the regime of which his father was a mainstay, Franco Farinacci had joined the anti-Fascist Italians fighting alongside the Allied armies; after the war, he resumed his diplomatic career. In the same way, while his father had remained an unrepentant Fascist, Luigi Barzini had also repudiated the regime. Following the liberation of southern Italy, Barzini had relaunched his career in Rome, initially as a journalist and publisher, then as writer and ultimately, a centre-right politician.

Emily had met Dodie Beatty during her time in Shanghai, and so she was amused to learn that the Englishwoman had turned up in Brisbane. Lorraine explained to Emily how she threaded her way through the minefield of her past with her new friend: 'I had to tread softly. I asked her news of her husband (*Bill*) … She told me they had divorced many years ago & he is interned up there. But she had no suspicion of me (*i.e. of having been a prostitute*)'.

Emily was the only person in whom Lorraine could confide her worries that her scarlet past would suddenly be thrown in her face, and their correspondence was a kind of therapy. And it wasn't only society's judgement that Lorraine agonised over; she judged herself, too. In her letters she continually repents of her past faults like 'bitchiness' and being a parasite ...

> *Looking back now on the China Days seems like a dream, sometimes unreal & sometimes a bit nightmarish ... Mickey, I often think how mean-spirited I used to be, and truly I've changed now, so don't hold all that against me, and the last few years have earned every penny myself …*

But she was gradually regaining her self-respect and equilibrium. Contributing to the war effort had given her a sense of having a place in society: 'I enjoy my role of respectability & am more or less useful member of the community – I could never be without work again'.

Emily responded positively: 'I am absolutely delighted with the tone of your letter. You sound so well-adjusted and happy and competent and new that I can't believe you're the same girl who used to live with me.'

There was, however, one aspect of their friendship that concerned Lorraine: Emily was writing about her.

The war had sparked a tremendous boom in reading. Deprived of most peacetime forms of diversion, often lonely, bored, scared or stuck in company they didn't want, women and men all round the world took refuge in books and magazines. The U.S. Government alone handed out 100 million free paperbacks to service personnel. As Emily said, it was 'a good age for writers' and now that her career as an author was back on track, she was eager to use the material she had acquired during her life in China – and Lorraine was part of it.

Emily's 'partial autobiography' *China to Me* was published in the United States in November 1944. Set against the dramatic background of the Sino-Japanese War and the occupation of Hong Kong, and with a wry commentary ranging across Chinese politics, gender relations and social mores, *China to Me* became a best seller. It canvassed prostitution, drug addiction, multiple partners, and interracial relationships; it even suggested that not all Japanese were sub-human fiends. This 'extreme frankness', one American reviewer commented, 'may unfortunately rule it out of school libraries'. Nevertheless *China to Me* sold over 700 000 copies and it made Emily a celebrity. When Charles Boxer was wrongly reported to have died in Japanese captivity in Hong Kong, these reports were published in Australian newspapers – not because he was famous, but because Emily was, thanks to the success of *China to Me*. As Lorraine told her, 'since your book your name is NEWS'.

The book's 'extreme frankness' testified to Emily's ruthless artistic method of using her own relationships as subject matter – often undisguised. For example, Boxer also featured in *China to Me* – and unlike Lorraine, under his real name. When he eventually managed to get hold of a copy, he was taken aback by the frankness and detail with which Emily had described their liaison.

'I never realized before just how elephantine your memory is,' Boxer wrote to her. 'I have been staggered to find myself confronted in print by fatuous remarks I have made at some drunken party.'

When *China to Me* came out in America, Emily warned Lorraine in general terms of what the book said about her. But it would be a full year before she could get her hands on an actual copy in Australia, and in the meantime she worried about what exactly it said, who might read it—and who might realise that she was Jean. Well before the book itself went on sale, excerpts appeared in the Australian press, and when Laura read in one of these that Emily had once lived near the Kiangse Road red light district, she grew agitated. She only calmed down when Lorraine told her that Boxer had promised to 'make an honest woman' of Emily by marrying her. As Lorraine explained to Emily, Laura and Australians generally saw things through 'small provincial eyes'.

But if Lorraine was concerned about *China to Me*, she had far more reason to worry about *Miss Jill*—if and when the novel appeared. She was only a minor character in *China to Me*, but Emily had foreshadowed that

> *I have written a whole book about Jean which a publisher is holding even now, waiting, he says, for the end of the war, "when people will be able to face realities". This sounds very grim, which Jean herself was not, but I suppose her life could be described by that adjective. At least it was grim in spots.*

By May 1945, Lorraine's job in Brisbane had come to an end and she was back in Sydney, living with her sister Margaret on the

North Shore and helping her with her young family.

Sydney was now host to another influx, this time of sailors from the British Pacific Fleet (BPF)—the expeditionary force which had been sent east to prosecute the war against Japan. The city's social alpinists jostled to welcome the BPF's upper class officers, the future Duke of Edinburgh among them—again, a minor theme of *Come In Spinner*. But in the eyes of many, the arrival of the British did not compensate for the departure of the better-paid Americans. 'It's been terrible here without the Yanks,' Lorraine said.

Germany's surrender brought only partial relief to war-weary Australians. It was assumed that the war against Japan would go on for a year or more and that, if the ongoing Battle of Okinawa was anything to go by, Allied casualties would be horrific. Lorraine was personally concerned because her brother John was in action again, taking part in the amphibious landings in Brunei in June. But now she had hit on a way of getting herself back to Asia, by signing up for the Women's Auxiliary Service Burma, an auxiliary organisation which provided canteen services for the British army fighting in Burma. She had got the job thanks to Dodie Beattie, who had also moved to Sydney, to work for the BPF. Dodie had given Lorraine a reference testifying to her 'Far East experience' and 'good character'.

But then, just as Lorraine was waiting for transport to Burma, the Pacific War ended. In 1940, her plans to escape from Australia had been thwarted by war. Now, they would be thwarted by peace.

II

'QUITE A STATE OF CONFUSION'

They wish now the war had just gone on and on … because they had a place there … and now they're scared because they haven't got one

George Johnston, *Clean Straw for Nothing*

FOR LORRAINE, as for many others, the end of the war came first as a moment of euphoria, then as an anti-climax, and then as a personal crisis.

For the victory celebration, Dodie had lined up dates for herself and Lorraine with two British naval officers. But the officers jilted them, handing them over to ordinary seamen, working class types from Yorkshire. Dodie was furious, saying that in pre-war Shanghai, 'she wouldn't think of knowing such people', and she was angry with Lorraine for accepting the situation and dancing with the Yorkies.

Dodie said she was 'awfully snobbish & said she knew it, but after all her husband was Indian Army'.

'Gee Mickey,' Lorraine told Emily, 'I nearly died at that.'

Dodie felt that, having been the wife of an officer, and thus a gentleman, she couldn't possibly break caste by dancing with lowly seamen. In light of Bill's subsequent career as bagman for a Shanghai knock shop, Lorraine thought this was ridiculous – but then she couldn't explain that to Dodie.

The victory party was soon over, and the reaction set in. We know a lot about Lorraine's state of mind around this time because a burst of correspondence between her and Emily has survived. The dynamic in their relationship pervades these post-war letters: Lorraine agonises over her status as an outcast; Emily reassures her that she has put the past behind her: 'I worried like anything about your future, and now I don't have to – nobody has to. You've mastered your fate.'

The writer George Johnston was a contemporary of Lorraine's. He had had an exciting, career-enhancing war and he was one of those in whom the anti-climax of peace triggered a personal crisis. So it's no accident that the quote at the head of this chapter, which comes from his novel *Clean Straw for Nothing*, captures Lorraine's state of mind precisely.

After years of feeling like an outsider, Lorraine's wartime work had given her a sense of self-worth, as well as a modicum of financial security. Finally, in her mid-thirties she had found her place – but now that sense of belonging had been swept away by the uncertainties of peace. She was 'in quite a state of confusion to say the least'.

And this 'state of confusion' wasn't just an existential condition – though it certainly was that – she worried about her economic security as well. 'For past three years I have enjoyed the security of Army jobs, with their billeting, food and amenities such as free travel etc. and no worry of insecurity,' she told Emily.

During the war, employment had been unavoidable, but now she had to compete for jobs in a market swamped by demobilising service personnel: 'naturally ex-army girls who've been in uniform get preference or else it is jobs for under 18 years of age as they get a lower basic wage'. For Lorraine, the obvious solution was marriage—just not to an Australian.

All her life Lorraine would have a love-hate relationship with the land of her birth and now, with the war over, hate came to the fore again. And being a foreigner, Emily offered a suitable ear for Lorraine's disdain:

> *Never under any circumstances come to Australia. I could never live here. It was O.K. in war time and whilst there was a war job to be done but in Peace Time it is the end of the world ... The men are so terribly masculine and can get along without women's company. They drink alone in the bars as women aren't permitted there, in fact they are rough and primitive and cannot be compared to your own countrymen or the nicer type of Englishmen.*

In the depths of her discontent, Lorraine turned again and again to the memory of her golden years in Shanghai, now 'congealed like a blood clot in her veins'. She recalled how, when she had been working with the American Army:

> *... some little private or corporal used to push me around and give me hell over any mistake I made. I'd think "why you little so-and-so, do you know who you are talking to? I was once a star at Madame Louise's, & if the Chinese saw you, you wouldn't even get upstairs ..."*

She might have been a whore—but at least she had been a high class one. Now her life was drab, symbolized by her lack of decent clothes: 'We are all shabby here as coupons don't go far and there is nothing decent to buy anyhow.'

And while the war had given her self-respect and comradeship, it had also taken years out of her life. So she was back to where she had been in 1931 and 1940: she badly wanted to get out of Australia – but now the obstacles were just as great, if not greater. Everywhere around the world, armies of service personnel and refugees were waiting to be repatriated, housed and absorbed back into the workforce. Even assuming Lorraine could find a job overseas she couldn't travel, as all available shipping berths were taken up for officially sanctioned purposes. She was going to need help.

Dodie Beatty had connections among business and official circles in China, and she offered to pull strings to get Lorraine a job in a British firm there. 'It's awfully nice of her really,' Lorraine told Emily, 'but I feel a bit scared of accepting' – scared that if she returned to Shanghai she would be outed as a prostitute. This was unlikely to happen in the United States, and so Lorraine asked Emily, who was now living in New York, to hire her as a nanny for Carola. Emily gently deflected Lorraine's request, softening her refusal with further compliments on her reform: 'I shall never cease wondering at the job you did on yourself.'

Meanwhile, Emily had herself attained respectability. Charles Boxer had arrived in New York in November 1945 and he and Emily got married three days later. When she heard the news, Lorraine made a point of assuring Emily that on his pre-war trips to Shanghai, Boxer had never visited Louise's brothel; it was her oblique way of saying that she had never slept with him.

A husband abroad could be a ticket out of Australia. During the war, thousands of Australian women had become married or engaged to Americans, and now these 'war brides' were given priority for berths on ships crossing the Pacific. If Lorraine could produce a fiancé in America, she might be able to join those women—and Harold Timperley, the journalist who had proposed to her three years before, was a candidate for the role.

Emily had run across Timperley in New York, where he was now working for the United Nations, and reported that he had just got divorced after a second brief marriage to a younger woman. Obviously not the stuff of which good husbands were made, Timperley nevertheless had other points to recommend him—for example, he was poised to get a job in the United Nations Relief and Rehabilitation Agency (UNRRA), which was in charge of post-war reconstruction efforts in China. So not only might he be able to get Lorraine out of Australia, he might even get her to China as well—if they were engaged. Emily reported that Timperley was

> *... sitting in his office looking backward and forward and being sentimental, not only about present work but about past marriage plans. He asked me if I had heard from you lately .... I wondered if he couldn't find something to bring you over ... I am pretty sure you could have Timperley again if you wanted him ... I'll keep* (him) *stirred up until I hear from you ...*

Lorraine replied that she was keen, but not that keen; she certainly did want to get married—but not to Timperley. All she wanted was a letter

> *from Timp. saying I was his fiancée then sailing would be easy as far as being able to get to U.S. Wives & fiancés are the only ones at present allowed to sail. I'm sure that he could find me some work and I wouldn't be a charge on anyone ... I will write a "friendly" letter to Timperley and feel my way with him'.*

But Timperley never replied to her 'friendly' letter and soon Emily was reporting that he was back in China, with a 'cushy job' in UNRRA. 'He always lands on his feet, that guy'.

Lorraine's gloom lifted when she got another job, back working for the Dutch NEI administration in Brisbane. In the wake of the Japanese surrender in Indonesia, there had been an upsurge of anti-colonial unrest, and the authorities were evacuating Dutch civilians to Australia. Lorraine's new job was as a welfare officer for these arriving refugees, so she went back to Brisbane and moved into a flat in Upper Edward Street in the city. Although it only lasted a few months, the arrangement cheered Lorraine up considerably, not least because she was sharing the flat with her friend Hazel Jones.

And it was now that Lorraine finally got her hands on a copy of *China to Me*. Although Emily had given her some idea of what to expect she, like Charles Boxer, was taken aback when confronted with her portrait in black and white. The book described her affair with Tokugawa, her career as an inmate in Louise's brothel, as a 'kept woman' and as a bisexual 'flibbertigibbet'; overall she comes across as a featherbrained hysteric, prone to theatrical suicidal gestures, who couldn't even finish a course in stenography. Lorraine told its author that the book had had quite an impact on 'my somewhat inflated ego'.

True, Emily had disguised Lorraine as Jean, but it was a pretty thin disguise. Anyone who knew of Lorraine's time with Tokugawa—who *was* named in the book—or who had been familiar with Emily's ménage in the Avenue Joffre, would have seen through it. Fortunately these were fairly small groups of people, and to throw everybody else off the track Lorraine had prepared a line of defence: that she knew for a fact that Jean was a foreigner on whom Emily had conferred Australian nationality. Lorraine tried out this defence on Hazel, insisting that Jean was really a New Zealander; the deception was accepted and Lorraine 'sighed with relief'. But we can be pretty certain Hazel didn't remain in ignorance for long.

Hazel now introduced Lorraine to another friend, Michele, who also worked for the Allied Intelligence Bureau. A Frenchwoman, she had lived with her family in Shanghai's French Concession and she had met Emily there. Hazel and Michele were also fans of Emily's books, so the three women had a lot in common. One night over dinner, they talked for hours about the world of *China to Me*. The story of an independent woman living and working in China, Emily's book struck a chord with this group, who were all keen to restart their expat lives. Hazel and Michele had been recruited by UNRRA and would soon be taking up new jobs in Shanghai. And all three knew Dodie Beatty, who thus became another topic of conversation.

While all these women were adjusting to the new post-war world, they judged that Dodie would find it hardest to cope because she was still wedded to the colonial privilege that wealthy Shanghailanders took as their due; as Lorraine put it: 'she is always living in the past & the time she was the spoilt beauty of Shanghai'. Among Dodie's unrealistic expectations was the belief that she was due a large sum in maintenance from her ex-husband Bill, even though it was a moot question whether he would be able to pay after years in a Japanese internment camp. And despite the fact that Dodie was so obviously well disposed to her, the fear that she would somehow learn that Lorraine was a former prostitute hadn't gone away. 'She worries me as I can't help thinking of Bill & Louise,' Lorraine told Emily, 'I hate living lies all the time.'

The threat was brought home when Dodie heard about

Lorraine's friendship with Michele. She wrote to warn her that Michele was not French at all but was in fact 'a White Russian from Avenue Joffre'—that is to say, a former prostitute. Dodie's cult of respectability existed in a bubble of self-delusion: here she was warning the ex-prostitute Lorraine against the suspected prostitute Michele, while waiting for an alimony payment from her ex-husband—derived from the earnings of prostitutes. Lorraine considered the situation 'amusing' and 'ironical', but it must have seemed to her that she would never escape the long shadow of the brothel on Connaught Road.

Emily's reaction was to tell her to stop dwelling on her past:

> *Yes, I know all about your reputation, but those things don't matter as they used to and even in the old days people with much more scarlet lives than you did it. You are so very different now anyway that nobody ought to think of you as the same person, although you were in many ways a very nice person even before your "reform" ...*

And she reassured Lorraine that their friendship was intact, and that they would one day meet again: 'I certainly would like to see you, as there are lots of things even now I don't like to put in letters and we would have several good laughs'.

Lorraine's brother John Murray was not one of those left stranded by the end of the war. Within hours of being discharged from the Army he was negotiating to purchase a sheep station in the far west region of New South Wales. The station, in the Cobar district, was called *Gidgee*, and Lorraine's other brother Peter Murray was managing an adjacent property. John took up the lease of *Gidgee* in partnership with Laura and his stepfather, and they moved out west. In February 1946, Lorraine joined them, and so the family was reunited for the first time since the turmoil following Chaffey's financial collapse, seventeen years before, had separated them. Lorraine's sister Margaret, her children and her husband, would soon also move to the far west.

The expansive landscape made a big impact on Lorraine, and in a letter to Emily she made life at *Gidgee* sound idyllic. 'Just off the homestead is a lagoon, with willows & white eucalyptus gum tree down on the banks. I love to walk there at sunset & watch myriads of "Gullahs" (*galahs, a species of cockatoo*) pink & grey parrots screech and fly down for their evening drink.' She forbore from mentioning the flies and the heat.

Lorraine's jobs included looking after the poultry and the vegetable garden and, rather than complaining about being forced to perform 'coolie work' she revelled in reconnecting with what she called her 'peasant & farmer' roots. These few months at *Gidgee* brought a closeness to her family and general sense of peace with the world which had long eluded her. To describe the regenerative effect, she reached back to her time in Shanghai:

> *Mickey, I remember years ago, during my Luigi period, when I was in hospital* (i.e. after her 1937 suicide attempt) *Luigi asked the priest what could be done, he told Luigi I needed to get close to the soil again & dig in the garden – it was only other day all the memories came back to me ... I'm certainly back to the Good Earth. To water the vegies etc, I go barefooted & feeling the soft red soil between my toes, I thought ... well I'm back more or less from where I started from, & I take naturally to this life ...*

The Good Earth was a 1931 novel by the American Pearl Buck, about a peasant family struggling to survive famine and war.

One of the most influential depictions of China ever to appear in the West, it won Buck the Nobel Prize for Literature and was made into an Academy Award-winning film. Lorraine's mention of it underlines the important part that reading played both in her life and her relationship with Emily: references to books—classics and new releases—pepper their correspondence. It was an aspect of their friendship that never waned. In one of Lorraine's last surviving letters to Emily, from the 1970s, she commented 'My reading of Victoriana has no end in sight'.

Lorraine's stay at *Gidgee* consolidated her relationship with her family. To give her a stake in their future prosperity, she was allotted 100 sheep from the family's flock, and her brothers told her that they would always be ready to support her. But she wasn't going to settle down in the far west: for one thing, she wanted to get married and Cobar didn't offer much in the way of eligible bachelors.

Her brothers semi-seriously suggested the owner of a neighbouring sheep station, a match which would bolster the family's position in the district. Then Lorraine attracted the eye of a wool classer (one who grades fleeces), but Laura quickly quashed that idea: 'not a wool classer, only a man of property'—not that Lorraine would have needed advice on that score. By now her plan was to travel to Britain to study physiotherapy and, in a further sign that the mother-daughter relationship was going through a good patch, Laura offered to support her to do this.

But however regenerative, her time at *Gidgee* could only be an interlude. It was 'great for a holiday, but I must be getting forth again in the world & make my own life, and a full life of work and achievement.' Lorraine concluded her despatch from *Gidgee* by apologising yet again to Emily for her behaviour in Shanghai: 'I just cannot understand how you or anyone else bothered with me, to put it mildly I must have been completely "nuts"'. And then, just as typically, 'please keep an eye out for an office job for me'.

This letter crossed with one from Emily, in which she described the bizarre finale to Lorraine's non-relationship with her former boss in Brisbane, Colonel Mapes. Out of the blue, Mapes had materialised at the Boxers' flat in New York and, in what must have been an excruciating and hilarious conversation, 'your Colonel' tried to enlist their support in persuading Lorraine to travel to the United States to become his mistress. It all sounded a bit messy; among the complications were the fact that Mapes was still married and that he was probably about to be sent to China to work for UNRRA. Emily cannily suggested that if Mapes could get Lorraine to China then that might swing the deal, but apparently this was beyond his powers.

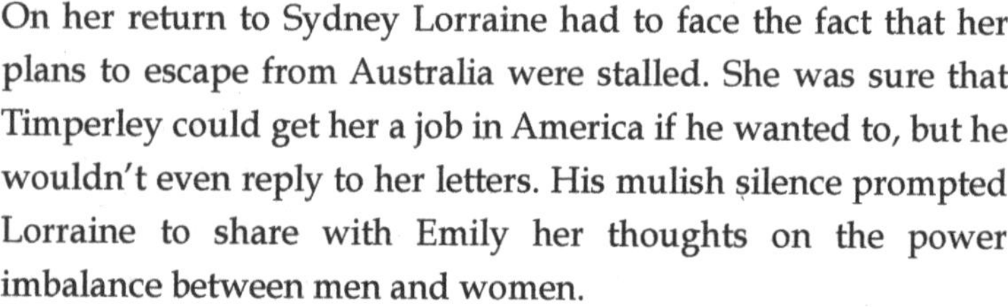

On her return to Sydney Lorraine had to face the fact that her plans to escape from Australia were stalled. She was sure that Timperley could get her a job in America if he wanted to, but he wouldn't even reply to her letters. His mulish silence prompted Lorraine to share with Emily her thoughts on the power imbalance between men and women.

Lorraine believed that the real reason Timperley was refusing to help her was because a job would have made her independent—and like all men, he didn't want women to be independent. And even if a woman were employed, their independence and job security was conditional on the need to be 'friendly' to the boss. In this respect, Lorraine argued, a sex worker was actually in a better and more straightforward position because the sexual contract was specified in advance. The office worker, in contrast, was dependent on the goodwill of the boss, and could be pressured into having sex without any return. 'See what I mean Mickey,' Lorraine said, 'men get the best deal all the time.'

Networking was a partial solution. Much to Lorraine's envy, Dodie Beatty's contacts in China had come through and she had landed a job in the British Consulate in Hankou. Over a few Pimms in the bar of the Australia Hotel off Martin Place, Dodie regaled Lorraine with her good fortune. Lorraine cattily observed that it was just as well that Dodie was on the way back to the land of personal servants, because she was looking distinctly 'moth-eaten'. This was unkind, particularly because Dodie offered to try and obtain a nominal offer of employment for Lorraine, which might help her get a passage to China where she could look for an actual job. But Lorraine was hesitant; as well as her old fear about being recognized as a former prostitute, she worried about landing in China without an actual job to go to: 'I'm an awfully conservative person these days & I know I couldn't ever adventure forth just on chance'. Her salad days were behind her.

And so Dodie sailed out of Sydney Harbour on a Royal Navy vessel, bound for Hong Kong. Their friendship had exemplified the ambivalent and bittersweet place that Shanghai held in Lorraine's life, where shame over her scarlet past vied with nostalgia at having lived in that glittering, romantic world. Gradually, nostalgia would gain the upper hand.

We catch only a few glimpses of Lorraine over the next year. She spent more time at *Gidgee*—in later years she would recall the golden winters of the far west region. Otherwise, she was in Sydney, living in her old wartime haunt of Potts Point and working as a typist in a legal office in the city.

While Lorraine was thus marking time, in August 1946 Emily

and Charles Boxer, together with their daughter Carola, moved from New York to England, where they moved into Boxer's family home in Dorset. And when their American nanny returned to the United States, Emily did Lorraine what was among the greatest of her many favours over the course of their long friendship: she gave her a job and advanced her the fare to England.

And so our next sight of Lorraine is in the British immigration records, disembarking in Southampton on 31 July 1947. She gave her age as 33, having finally settled on 1914 as the year of her birth.

III

CONYGAR

Captious is the word for Lorraine

Emily Hahn, *England to Me*

LORRAINE HAD now reached a time of life when many people feel that their horizons are closing in, but for her it was the opposite: they were opening out. These were the best years of her life, the years when her dreams came true.

Not everyone was so lucky. Living conditions in Britain were in some ways not much better than they had been in wartime. In trying to hang on to its empire and status as a Great Power, the country was spending 15% of GDP on defence, at a time when the Labour Government was also committed to an ambitious domestic program, including the introduction of the National Health Scheme. The country was nearly bankrupt and the government had slashed the value of the pound. The previous winter had been one of the coldest on record, cutting industrial and agricultural production. Food rationing continued, and a recurring topic of Lorraine's letters home would be the parcels dispatched by Laura from food-rich Australia to the Boxer household.

The Boxers lived at *Conygar*, a mock-Tudor mansion set in extensive grounds outside the village of Broadmayne in Dorset.

As a residence, the house left something to be desired; it had been taken over by the military during the war and was in a ruinous state – every single bathroom fitting was broken. On the other hand, living in rural Dorset softened the impact of food rationing: a large vegetable garden ensured that there was plenty of parsnip and potato on the menu.

Conygar was full of Chinese antiques which had been looted in Beijing during the Boxer Rebellion by one of Charles Boxer's relatives and of which, Lorraine said, he was 'ashamed'. There were literary associations, too. Thomas Hardy's house *Max Gate*, where the novelist lived until his death in 1928, was just up the Dorchester road and the baker in Broadmayne could remember delivering the great man's daily bread order. Further to the north lay the moorland of Exmoor, which Lorraine called '*Lorna Doone* country' after the Victorian novel set there.

When Lorraine arrived, both Emily and Charles were hard at work. Emily, as always, was writing for *The New Yorker* and had several books in hand. Charles had left the Army and was on his way to establishing himself as one of the Anglophone world's leading historians of early European, and particularly Portuguese, colonialism. He had recently accepted the Chair of Portuguese History and Literature at Kings College at the University of London and one of Lorraine's duties would be typing his manuscripts, along with *Conygar's* administrative correspondence. In the coming year, she would work hard around the house, though she was treated as one of the family rather than an employee.

In 1950, Emily would publish another memoir entitled *England to Me* which gives Lorraine a whole chapter to herself – and this time she was called by her real name. Titled 'Australian in the

Henhouse', the chapter is a long funny story about Lorraine taking charge of *Conygar*'s chickens. Using the skills she had gained looking after the chickens at *Gidgee* Lorraine experiments with different types of feed, along the way competing for the kitchen scraps with the estate caretaker, who wants them for his pigs. Finally she manages to persuade the finnicky English birds to start laying—only to be robbed of the fruits of victory when the cook appropriates all the eggs.

It's a country house comedy in which Lorraine—'an old friend of mine from Australia'—is an utterly different character to the Jean of *China to Me*, let alone the Jill of *Miss Jill*. Nothing connects her to them. There is no mention of a scarlet past; indeed, no mention that she had ever been to China. Instead of the parasitic Jean, Lorraine is a diligent—perhaps overly diligent—help around the house. Her prevailing vice is no longer frivolity but something like the opposite: she has become serious.

> *I hadn't realized how much emphasis Lorraine placed on being Australian ... the experience of the war had put the colonial iron into her soul ... She says the Aussies were wildly fond of the Americans, who arrived just when people were terribly jittery because aid was not coming from England but when I begin to swell with pride ... she reminds me tartly how much more of the brunt England bore in Europe than the United States did. She goes into a rage if she is called English; she also goes into a rage if anyone says Princess Elizabeth's living allowance ought to be cut. She says Australia is terribly provincial, and then she complains that the farms in England are too small .... Captious is the word for Lorraine ...*

'Australian in the Henhouse' is a good example of Emily's habit of drawing on her surroundings – whether war-torn China or the English counties – for material for her writing, grist for her ever-turning mill. But it also marks a sea change in the way Emily saw Lorraine: she was now hard working, conscientious, and a good nanny to Carola.

In early October, Boxer and Emily went to the Netherlands for a week and while they were away, Lorraine looked after Carola. It was during this time that Lorraine met Ann Latch, a war widow who lived nearby and whose daughter Rose, was a school friend of Carola's. By the end of her stay at *Conygar,* Lorraine would be describing Mrs Latch as a 'true and sincere friend' – and this was another friendship which would last for decades.

Rose – now Rose Knox-Peebles – remembers Lorraine at this time as:

> *... remarkably pretty – she had a little, cat-shaped face and I think her hair was in a bob. She had an Australian accent which added to the mystique. She played with Carola and me a lot, which was nice for us – she was great fun and was very approachable whereas Micky and Charles (Emily and Boxer) were rather grand and very clever and shut away in their studies... (they) only appeared at mealtimes when they read books, propped on bookstands ...*

She has vivid memories of *Conygar.*

> *Neither Charles nor Mickey drove, but Carola and I could walk across the downs to each other's houses. The Boxer's house was always filled with (to my young eyes) vey exotic people – a lot of women in Saris, black doctors, Japanese academics – it was the most amazing place.*

Another of Emily's topics in *England to Me* was 'the new democratic order of things in Changing England'. She was referring to the radical reforms introduced by the Attlee Labour government, but England would prove quite resistant to change. As Lorraine wrote to Laura:

> *Sometimes I think how like this life here is like my life in China, and it all boils down to the fact that we have servants ... Charles caught me polishing my shoes recently in the shoe room, and he was quite mad at me, as he said it was Jan's job* (Jan was a servant, a Polish refugee) *and I'd only lose face if I did so many things for myself, but you know it is so hard having people wait on one after being so independent in Australia.*

Austerity Britain was a study in contrasts. Food rationing put unpalatable dishes like whale and snoek (barracoota) on the dining table, and Emily and Lorraine struggled to cater for dinner parties when the only available ingredients were different types of tinned meat and the ubiquitous parsnips. On the other hand, thanks to the Boxers' connections, Lorraine was moving in 'good' society, the county aristocracy of Dorset, and her letters to Laura are full of knights and dames, generals and admirals. She sat next to the son of Field Marshal Montgomery at the South Dorset Hunt Ball. Then, like her brothers had at *Gidgee*, Charles Boxer began to semi-seriously propose a husband for Lorraine – a widowed general of his acquaintance. But she wasn't interested.

From *Conygar*, she made occasional trips to London. Having last visited the city before the Blitz, she was struck by the bombed-out ruins and also by the fact that the streets were full of 'foreigners' – by which she meant Europeans, many of them Polish refugees. To celebrate her birthday, in January 1948 Charles and Emily took Lorraine up to London where they had lunch at the Savoy, drinks at the Ritz and dinner at the Café Royale; the guests included Portuguese and Chinese diplomats. Afterwards, Lorraine stayed on for a few days and she started dropping into the reading room at the High Commission, Australia House, where she could read the *Australian Women's Weekly*, the magazine which was the bible of Australian women of her generation. Because only Australians were allowed into the reading room, the men who frequented it saw any women there as fair game, and she resented the presumption.

Her opinion of Australian men had not improved. 'What so many of our chaps are doing in London I can't imagine, they always look like plumbers ... their suits badly cut and sloppy compared to the English.' Australians stood out not just because of their clothes but because they were the only men wearing Returned Soldier's badges. As Lorraine explained to her mother, Britain had not issued such badges to ex-service personnel because the authorities took the view that the whole population had been on the front line—far more British civilians died in the war than did Australian soldiers. As a result the government decided not to single out the military in this way.

Over the years, Lorraine's politics moved around a lot. In the 1930s she was pro-Japanese and pro-Italian Fascist, then during the Pacific War she became ardently patriotic and anti-Fascist. After the war, she moved through various phases: stridently anti-communist, deeply conservative, moderately liberal, and strongly feminist—and eventually she wound up hailing the advent of Margaret Thatcher. These shifts tended to reflect her changing circles of acquaintance over the course of a long lifetime. And now the dramatic advent of the Cold War—and the influence of her mentors Emily and Charles—made a deep impression on her.

In the 1930s, Emily, along with many others in her liberal circle, had 'approved' of communism; she had not been a diehard supporter but might have been considered, in the jargon of the day, a 'fellow traveller'. But by the early 1940s she had definitely turned against Marxism; one result was that her friendship with the communist activist Agnes Smedley turned to hostility. In thus distancing herself from the hard Left, Emily was slightly ahead of a broad shift in the mood among the Western democracies. The end of the wartime alliance with Moscow, and the brutal imposition of Soviet-backed regimes in Eastern Europe, turned public opinion generally against communism.

In early 1948, the new Republic of Italy was preparing to hold its first parliamentary elections. There were fears that a strong electoral showing by the left-wing *Fronte Democratico Popolare* might prompt a Soviet-backed takeover—as had actually occurred just months before in Czechoslovakia. The newly founded American CIA threw its weight behind Italy's right-wing *Democrazia Cristiana* party, funding their candidates and running dirty tricks campaigns against the FDP, helping the Christian Democrats to a decisive victory.

'Wonderful news about the Italian elections, and the Commos being defeated,' Lorraine wrote to Laura. 'It meant so much to us all here ... rather like the Munich days'. To the residents of *Conygar,* the elections had recalled the dramatic events of the Munich Agreement because they believed that fate of Europe had lain in the balance—with the difference that, unlike in 1938, freedom had triumphed over the totalitarian threat. But only two months later the Soviet Union imposed its blockade of Berlin, triggering the first major confrontation of the Cold War.

Meanwhile, *Conygar* continued to receive its stream of exotic visitors. One was Charles Drage, who in the 1930s had been the head of the Secret Intelligence Service in Hong Kong, where he had been a colleague of Charles Boxer, then in Military Intelligence. Now, Drage had taken up a new position with the British Council in London, and he and his wife invited Lorraine to stay with them there.

Another visitor was the Australian journalist Dorothy Jenner, who was currently in the UK on assignment for Lorraine's old employer the Sydney *Sun*. Like Emily and Charles Boxer, Jenner had been in Hong Kong when it had been overrun by the Japanese, and like Emily's character Miss Jill, she had been locked up in the civilian internment camp at Stanley. This was a coincidence, because the novel *Miss Jill* had now, finally, been launched into print.

IV

The Making of Miss Jill

Could one really reform, Jill asked herself, after such a sin as she had been committing all these years?

Emily Hahn, *Miss Jill*

NINE YEARS after Emily had finished its first draft, *Miss Jill* was published in the United States in November 1947.

Her aim in writing the novel was to comment about society and prostitution, about gender relations and hypocrisy, and to do that she took Lorraine's life and fictionalised it. As a result, Jill is somewhat loosely based on Lorraine and, unlike Jean in *China to Me,* she is often portrayed as a pawn and a victim.

When the novel opens, Jill, about twenty years old, is working in a high class Shanghai brothel. The daughter of a promiscuous and neglectful mother and an unknown father, as a teenager Jill had been picked up on a Sydney beach by a Japanese nobleman. He took her abroad and began a sexual relationship with her, which ended when his wife's powerful family had Jill thrown out of Japan. Then, passing through Shanghai on her way home to Australia, she was seduced by a pimp who trafficked her into the sex industry.

In the brothel, Jill attracts the interest of a Chinese businessman who supports her to leave the industry, setting her up in a comfortable flat. He encourages her to study stenography, which will enable her to earn a normal living. Although Jill craves the respectability and social acceptance an office job would bring, she struggles to leave her past as a prostitute behind her. She becomes disillusioned with 'normal' life. Business school proves both demanding and boring. The disappointments mount up: she begins a relationship with an American journalist, only to find that he has lied to her about his marriage.

So far the story approximately follows the course of Lorraine's own life down until 1938—the major difference being that Jill is six or seven years younger than Lorraine was when she traced this path. Then at this point, the setting of the novel shifts to Hong Kong in the period before and during the Pacific War. Lorraine herself only ever spent a few weeks in Hong Kong, and so for the geographical and historical setting of this part Emily drew on her own experience in the British colony. Despite this change of setting, the narrative arc of the novel—Jill's faltering progress towards 'reform'—continues to follow Lorraine's story.

In Hong Kong, Jill goes back to working in a brothel before, again, being bought out of sex work by another philanthropic businessman. When the Japanese occupy the colony in December 1941, she at first becomes the mistress of a Japanese officer and is then sent to the Stanley internment camp, and it is here that Jill completes her journey to reform. Hitherto, she had felt excluded from society not just because of her fear of being judged by others, but also because she had judged *herself* unworthy. But the harsh life in the camp reduces the inmates to a common level of deprivation and obliterates distinctions of social rank. In this new environment of shared adversity, Jill finds herself: she helps other people, is taken on her merits, becomes accepted and even liked.

And now she gets religion. In the Stanley camp she meets the

Catholic priest Father Sullivan, under whose spiritual guidance she finds peace and self-acceptance. The novel ends with Jill watching the arrival of the British fleet sent to retake control of Hong Kong, looking forward to living a worthy life, sustained by her new found faith.

It's an uplifting ending that strikes the reader as abrupt and unconvincing—and quite unlike Lorraine's own experience.

In *China to Me*, Emily tells how when Lorraine moved into her Avenue Joffre house in early 1938, 'we soon set to work on a book, the story of her life'. The *we* is significant; at this point Lorraine was a willing collaborator, but in the years ahead, the knowledge that she would be portrayed, and the fear that she would be identified, as a prostitute weighed more and more heavily on her.

Emily had sent a draft of *Miss Jill* to her New York publisher by late 1938 but they sat on it, worried that if it were published, its frank treatment of prostitution might taint Emily's image among the reading public. Six years later, the manuscript was still sitting in her publisher's bottom drawer.

We get a glimpse of this early version in a letter Emily wrote to Lorraine in June 1945, in which she describes it as 'as a record of somebody we knew long ago—an interesting sociological study. But alas poor girl she died long before Pearl Harbour'. This detail—that the heroine dies before Pearl Harbour—tells us that the Hong Kong chapters had yet to be added. Lorraine said in her reply that she had always been sure that her character 'would have come to a sticky end'—a light-hearted comment which masked her continuing anxiety about the book.

Some months later, Lorraine received a letter from her admirer Colonel Mapes, who said that he had just read *China to Me* and that he had had no difficulty in identifying Jean as Lorraine. Given that she had told him about her way of life in Shanghai this was unsurprising, but Mapes also said he was looking forward to 'the further adventures of Jean'—which suggests that Lorraine had told him that Emily had also written a novel about her. Mapes' letter raised Lorraine's anxiety to a new level, and she asked Emily to hold off from publishing until she had managed to get out of Australia. Once she had escaped the parochial confines of Sydney, she explained, she wouldn't have to care about 'what is said about me'.

Emily's response was twofold. First, she played down the possibility of the novel ever being published at all, and then, even if it was, the danger of Lorraine being recognized as the model for Jill ...

> *Sorry old Mapes penetrated our disguise, but you must have told him a good deal about yourself already. Don't worry about the book. I mean your book; at the moment there is not the slightest prospect of it ever coming out and if and when it does I shall rewrite it thoroughly, making it completely fictional. I cross my heart that nobody would ever be able to connect it up with you ...*

Second, she addressed the underlying problem of Lorraine's insecurity:

> *It doesn't matter how many people know about you* (i.e. having been a prostitute) ... *Nowadays nobody gives a damn ... It's all in the way you think about yourself and if you go right ahead as if you knew what you are doing and are quite sure of it, you'll find that other people don't like to start anything ...*

It was good advice, if easier to give than to take.

And while Lorraine worried about the threat of exposure that Emily's books posed, she also took pride in her fame as a character—even if only as a disguised character—in those books. She told Emily how someone she knew had bought a copy of *China to Me* in the United States, and that the shop assistant had boasted that she herself had lived in Shanghai, that she had known Emily and Jean—and that she knew for a fact that Jean was currently living in the States. Lorraine commented tartly on this presumption.

Emily had that key quality of the successful author: she was prolific. By early 1946 she was working on several projects including some children's books, an extended account of her time in Hong Kong and a biography of Sir Stamford Raffles, the founder of Singapore. Professionally it was shaping up to be a good year, but in terms of financial return she judged that these books 'won't pay off as well as *China to Me*'. The book which had introduced Lorraine to the reading public, albeit as only a minor figure, had been a big success, and now Emily was keen to repeat that success with *Miss Jill*.

In a letter in late April, Emily returned to the subject of her novel, reassuring Lorraine that:

> *I've quite given up the idea of using that manuscript as it is. I think instead I will do a fictional pseudo-psychological book about a prostitute in the Far East based not on Jean, whose career is simply unbelievable anyway, but on the more ordinary sort of tart I had a good look at coming back on the Gripsholm* (the ship on which Emily and other American civilians had been repatriated in 1943) *Not nearly so glamorous but much truer to life. .... I think you*

> *will admit that Jean, who you knew pretty well, was not typical at all. She was in a class by herself ... some of her surroundings, yes, and some of the things she heard about her pals might do, but not her own career.*

But Emily never got around to this wholesale revision of the manuscript. When the novel finally did appear Jill *was* recognisably Jean—and to those few in the know, Jean *was* recognisably Lorraine. Instead of completely transforming the main character from an ingénue into a 'more ordinary sort of tart', Emily simply added the Hong Kong portion, including, crucially, Jill's 'reform'.

'A story of salvation and sin': this blurb on the cover of *Miss Jill* invoked the idea that fallen women could be 'reformed' by repenting and beginning a new and virtuous life. This was a key tenet of evangelical Christianity, and one vigorously promoted by powerful lobby groups in America, Britain and Australia. Even wicked Shanghai had a Moral Welfare League, which had had enough influence in the 1920s to obtain a ban on brothels in the International Settlement—though as Madam Louise's thriving establishment on Connaught Road showed, this had little practical effect.

Though she had constantly urged Lorraine to make a new and more worthwhile life for herself, Emily was deeply sceptical about the evangelical baggage of the idea of 'reform'. And so, when she uses 'reform' in the context of their relationship—for example, in her account of Jean, or in her letters to Lorraine—she does so in an ironic, subversive way. But when it came to writing *Miss Jill*, she found it necessary to defer to the prevailing Christian morality.

The conventional, evangelical idea of reform was enshrined in the works of the 19th century novelists so beloved by Lorraine and Emily. In *Miss Jill*, Emily quotes from an episode in Charles Dickens' *David Copperfield*, the scene where the hero comes across the 'fallen' Martha Endell bewailing her degradation on the banks of the foetid Thames:

> *'Oh, the river! … I know it's like me! ... It comes from country places, and it creeps through the dismal streets, defiled and miserable – and it goes away, like my life, to a great sea, that is always troubled … I am bad, I am lost. I have no hope at all' ...*

This was a classic expression of the shame that 'fallen' women were expected to feel, and Jill identifies so strongly with Martha that she bursts into tears. And as it turns out, Copperfield has turned up just in time to prevent Martha from throwing herself into the river. He puts her on the path to reform, and she will eventually be rewarded by marriage – although as penance she has to go and live in Australia.

The feminist in Emily ridiculed these attitudes. In *China to Me*, she mocks the Copperfields of the day, the 'earnest young men' who regularly tried to persuade Lorraine to take up the life of a virtuous and marriageable (if low-paid) stenographer. But as an author Emily (and her publisher) was aiming at a prospective audience for *Miss Jill*, Middle America, which was deeply conventional. She rewrote the manuscript so that, unlike the 'grim' ending of the earlier version, Jill 'reforms', and does so under the guidance of a male saviour, the Catholic priest Father Sullivan.

Emily must have hoped that with this bow to convention, *Miss Jill* would be picked up by the movie industry. And she could have expected that the setting and subject matter would help, because what Paris was to romance, Shanghai was to prostitution.

Passing through Shanghai in the 1930s, the celebrated Hollywood director Joseph von Sternberg had taken Emily out to lunch. Von Sternberg had already used the city as a setting in his Oscar-winning *Shanghai Express,* starring Marlene Dietrich, who proclaims her profession with the immortal words 'It took more than one man to change my name to Shanghai Lily'. He used it again in *The Shanghai Gesture,* starring Gene Tierney as a privileged young woman fatally corrupted by the city's immorality. Von Sternberg's proven success with the theme and setting would have reinforced Emily's hope that a novel about Shanghai prostitute stood a good chance of being turned into a movie.

But although republished several times, *Miss Jill* did not repeat the success of *China to Me* and it never made it onto the screen. One reason was that by the time the book appeared in 1947, public attitudes in the United States were more censorious than they had been when Emily had first conceived of the book a decade earlier.

These attitudes were embodied in the Motion Picture Production Code (known as the Hays Code after its author William Hays). This prohibited depictions or allusions on-screen to a wide range of topics including prostitution, adultery and inter-racial sex, and its influence wasn't confined to cinemas. For example, because of its 'immorality' Kathleen Winsor's 1944 novel *Forever Amber*, the story of a courtesan in Restoration England, was banned in fourteen American states—and outright in Australia. In order to get *Forever Amber* onto the screen, 20th Century Fox had to dramatically tone down the sex, and even in this sanitised form it provoked the Hays Code Administrators into tightening their rules. The message was clear: if you hoped that your novel might possibly be turned into a movie, then you wrote, as it were, with Mr Hays looking over your shoulder.

Seen in this light, another of the blurbs for *Miss Jill* seemed like an appeal to the censors to focus on its revised, more moral ending:

> *Degraded beyond imagination, she dared not hope for redemption ... There is pity in the agonised struggles of Miss Jill from Shanghai as she cried for love in a world of violence and lust – but there is purity also, and strength, and an affirmation of spiritual virtue ...*

But if Emily hoped that Jill's 'reform' would deflect criticism from her novel, she was wrong.

In America, the reaction to *Miss Jill* was lukewarm at best. The *New York Herald Tribune* commented that Emily's material 'seems to get a bit out of hand' and the *Saturday Review of Literature* went further, condemning the novel as 'the prank of an enfant terrible'. It was better received in Britain. 'Miss Jill is as pleasant company and as solid a personality as Moll Flanders, and the fact that there is no attempt to whitewash and falsify her makes her adventures the more moving', said *The Times Literary Supplement*.

In the novel, Emily made more of an effort to obscure the originals of characters than she had in *China to Me*. For example, in her memoir Tokugawa Iemasa had been identified by name – when it was published in the middle of the Second World War there had been no need to spare the blushes of any Japanese. But in *Miss Jill*, he becomes the anonymous 'Botchan', and there was a good reason why this should be so.

Tokugawa's eminence had increased: on the death of his father Prince Iesato, he had inherited both the latter's title and his seat in the House of Peers. Despite this, during the war Tokugawa had kept his distance from the militarist regime and in 1946, with the approval of the American Occupation authorities, he took his father's old position as President of the House of Peers. As such, he was an important figure in the transition to a new Japanese democracy. The Americans' nation-building strategy depended partly on maintaining the prestige of the Chrysanthemum Throne, and exposing the uncle-by-marriage of the Empress to ridicule by mentioning him in a salacious novel wouldn't have helped.

And yet, however much Emily toned things down, she wasn't discreet enough. At one point in *Miss Jill*, Madam Annette suggests to Jill that she should take a break from Shanghai and go and work as a prostitute somewhere else in Asia. They mull over the possibilities—Tientsin (now Tianjin), Hong Kong, Honolulu, and Singapore—and then Annette says 'There's always the Sultan of Johore'. This was a throwaway line which didn't go down well with the Sultan of Johore.

In 1938, the Sultan had divorced his Scottish wife in order to make way for the English cabaret dancer Cissie Hill. In 1940, Hill was killed when a stray German bomb hit a luxury furrier's shop in Kent; less than a month later the Sultan married *her* successor, a Rumanian forty-two years his junior. Perhaps unsurprisingly, when the Sultan's London lawyers learnt of the reference in *Miss Jill* to their esteemed client they threatened to sue; a threat which halted the novel's distribution in the UK. In response to this, and in the hope of a wider audience, *Miss Jill* was toned down even further for the revised paperback edition which appeared in 1950. All mention of the Sultan was removed.

Miss Jill wasn't released in Australia until December 1948, and there, too, its reception was less than positive. One reviewer in the *West Australian* revealed a lot about local prejudices by assuming that Jill must be Anglo-Indian. It was unthinkable to white Australians that an Anglo-Celtic woman would voluntarily lower herself to work in a brothel that catered to Asian customers. In order to submit to such an indignity they had to be 'shanghaied' – drugged and kidnapped. On the other hand, women of mixed Indian origin were deemed to be innately promiscuous.

These attitudes were rooted in Australians' belief in their racial superiority, mixed with anxiety over what they saw as their geopolitical isolation. The *West Australian* made the connection between these two delusions explicit by commenting that *Miss Jill* was set in the region that was known in Britain 'as the Far East, but is much too close to us'. One Sydney reviewer spelt it out: Jill's real sin was not prostitution as such, but having sex with Asians. However, they felt that one aspect of *Miss Jill* made it fit for public consumption: 'Australian honour is saved, however, when she turns heroine in an internment camp. Gets virtuous, too'. Emily's conventional ending had appeased one critic at least.

Miss Jill got a new lease of life in the late 1950s. By now, the influence of the Hays Code was weakening, and publishers decided they could get away with emphasising sin rather than salvation. One paperback edition, seeking to cash in on the success of Richard Mason's 1957 novel *The World of Suzie Wong*, compared Jill to its prostitute heroine. But this shift in standards came too late for Emily's novel. Shanghai had ceased to be 'the Whore of the Orient' and *Miss Jill* had missed its chance of capitalising on the city's former reputation.

To the extent that there *was* a David Copperfield in Lorraine's life it was Emily herself. But the publication of *Miss Jill* marked the definitive end of the first phase of their relationship. Previously there had been an imbalance between the insecure former sex worker and the assured and successful writer, between the 'flibbertigibbet' and the mentor. From now on, their friendship would more and more be one between equals.

Five: Wunsy
Dorset 1948 – London 1974

… loved her very much in his eccentric way
Emily Hahn, *China to Me*

I

AT LAST

he really hasn't changed
Lorraine Murray on her reunion with Edmund Toeg

EDMUND AND Lorraine had stayed in touch after he had stopped paying her an allowance, and they continued to write to each other even after the Japanese, in 1943, moved most of the foreign population of Shanghai's International Settlement, Edmund among them, into internment camps. But the link was a tenuous one: in October 1945, two months after the internees had been freed, Lorraine mentioned to Emily that she had yet to receive any word from him.

At this point, six years after they had last set eyes on each other, it seems like Lorraine had almost given up on Edmund. Referring to their fantasy relationship, she told Emily, 'I've certainly outgrown that "Wunsy, Dee Dee" set up, and have no desire to take it up again. My grey hairs would probably do the trick, as he liked "little girls".' Yet when next she mentions Edmund, two years later, she was bent on marrying him.

At some stage Edmund had suffered a 'nervous breakdown', and when Lorraine arrived at *Conygar* in July 1947 he was still in Shanghai and not replying to her letters. But despite this silence, the prospects of her marrying Edmund were actually improving because the strict mores of Shanghailander society were melting away, and as they did, so too did many of the obstacles to their relationship.

The Sino-Japanese War was over but the Chinese Civil War, pitting the Kuomintang against the Chinese Communist Party, was gathering pace. The International Settlement and the French Concession had been handed back to China, a development which had stripped the Shanghailanders of the legal basis of their privilege, and when the city fell to the communists in 1949 they would lose what was left of their financial foothold. There was an exodus of British, Europeans and Americans seeking to resettle elsewhere—enough so that the American immigration authorities used a special term, the 'China Whites', to describe them. Edmund's mother Sophia and sister Nora had already moved to Los Angeles and his younger sister Dora and her son had joined them there from Greece, while the younger brother David, who was married to a White Russian, remained in Shanghai. It was assumed Edmund would join his womenfolk in California, but it wasn't clear when.

Hitherto Lorraine's relations with the family had been delicate, to say the least, but by now she had struck up a correspondence with Nora, whose sisterly diagnosis was that Edmund 'just can't make the effort to leave China after all these years there'. He was displaying the attachment to familiar surroundings—or the inertia—which would become more and more pronounced in the years to come.

Meanwhile another key member of the clan, Sir Victor Sassoon, was passing through London, and he invited Lorraine to lunch. Sir Victor, of course, knew all about Lorraine's scarlet life in Shanghai, and she must have been nervous when she arrived at his hotel: their meeting would be a test of whether she would be accepted by the Shanghailander community at large. She passed the test easily, Sassoon treating her with great consideration, showing himself 'very interested' in her first-hand account of the Australian wool industry. At their parting he gave her a present, an envelope containing £25 – the equivalent of approximately £800 today.

Sassoon was about to return to China, where he would spend the coming year attempting, with scant success, to liquidate his Shanghai property and transfer the proceeds overseas. Ultimately he would lose his Chinese investments, but he had enough left in his global portfolio to sustain a plutocrat's lifestyle. In fact of all the foreigners dislodged from Shanghai, the wealthy members of the Baghdadi Jewish community were among the more fortunate. The less fortunate – such as the former rank and file of the Shanghai Municipal Police – faced a more uncertain future. But even they were better off than the White Russians, many of whom trustingly accepted Soviet offers of repatriation to their homeland, only to be sent to the Gulag on arrival.

Yet even for the wealthy Baghdadis it was a wrench to leave Shanghai. Around this time another of the Toeg clan, Solomon Toeg, died in Shanghai, and Edmund's mother wrote offering her condolences to his widow Hannah. In her reply Hannah evoked the sense of dislocation among their community: 'The poor man went through a lot in the last 10 years … Life is so full of sorrows perhaps he is at peace in a better world. What great changes are taking place in our lives we are all drifting apart & I wish it were not so.'

But it was this very sense that they were drifting apart that prompted these emigrés, once they had found new homes outside China, to stick together. Two of Hannah Solomon's sons were already established in Britain (a third had died during the war while serving with the RAF) and one of these, Victor Toeg, would act as Edmund's lawyer in the years ahead.

Edmund finally joined his mother and sisters in Los Angeles in December 1947.

By now it wasn't just Lorraine who thought that she and Edmund should get married. Emily and Charles Boxer were also in favour of the match, and they invited Edmund to come and stay at *Conygar*. And if he wouldn't come to Lorraine, the Boxers had a plan B: they were intending to visit the United States during the summer academic break and offered to take Lorraine with them, so that she would be able to run him to ground in America. Sir Victor Sassoon also approved of a match between his eccentric cousin and Lorraine. He kept a benevolent eye on her from afar, sending her another £25 for her birthday and, when he found out that Emily had advanced Lorraine her fare from Australia, he reimbursed his old lover. 'Isn't he wonderful,' cooed Lorraine.

It seemed everyone was in favour of their marriage—except perhaps Edmund, who hadn't actually proposed to her. But at least now he was writing to her again. Accounting for his last two years in Shanghai, he told Lorraine how, giving up the forex brokerage business, he had immersed himself in the study of Chinese antiques. These scholarly labours had not been entirely disinterested: having liquidated such assets as he could in Shanghai, he used his new expertise to buy a stock of Chinese *objets d'art*. Unlike real estate or large sums of hard currency, these could quite easily be taken out of China—as long as one got around the ban on exporting them, something Edmund managed to do. It was a characteristically shrewd financial decision, and his antiques would appreciate considerably in value over the next few decades.

After some months of vacillation, Edmund decided to travel to Britain. But following his nervous breakdown, rumours were circulating about his state of mind: Emily had heard that he was 'very changed' from pre-war days and that his conversation was 'rambling'. Against this worrying background, Lorraine received a letter from Nora, one which indicated her future standing among the Toegs. Nora wielded the authority of the oldest child over her younger siblings and from now on she would treat Lorraine as one of those.

To encourage Edmund to settle in England, Charles Boxer had offered to help him find an academic position lecturing on Chinese antiquities—but Nora vetoed the proposal. She instructed Lorraine 'to discourage any plans he has of wanting to lecture as his brain should not be overtired with such things'. And she directed Lorraine to set Edmund up in some quiet place, like a country village, and arrange for a housekeeper to look after him.

But Lorraine had her own plans for Edmund.

At last, on 21 April 1948, he disembarked at Southampton. He arrived at *Conygar* in some style, having hired two cars to ferry his luggage, including several years' supply of soap—which was heavily rationed in Britain. It was nearly nine years since Wunsy and Dee Dee had last seen each other but she thought he looked well: 'except for his hair gone grey at temples and a bit thinner he really hasn't changed'. He settled in at *Conygar*—whose rural quiet made it 'an ideal spot for anyone recovering from a breakdown'. Hazel Jones, the great friend Lorraine had made in Brisbane, was visiting and the trio went for long walks in the grounds.

Edmund brought news of another old friend, Lorraine's dog Jaime, who had wound up in Italy in the care of Admiral Alberto Da Zara. Da Zara was an old China hand and a famed womaniser—he had an affair with Wallis Simpson during her time in Beijing—and he had somehow acquired Jaime in

Shanghai. During World War II, Da Zara had proved one of Italy's more successful admirals; he and Jaime, who went everywhere with him, had seen plenty of action against the British Navy in the Mediterranean. Now, two old seadogs, they were living in retirement.

But even long walks in the Dorset countryside couldn't bring Edmund up to the point of proposing to Lorraine, and the Boxers' offer of a trip to the United States remained open. So on 11 June 1948, the *SS America* steamed out of Southampton bound for New York carrying the Boxers and Lorraine, travelling as Carola's nanny. Her departure seemed to have the required effect on Edmund.

Three weeks later Lorraine was on an aircraft, one of the new Lockheed Constellations, bound from New York to Los Angeles. Sitting a few seats away was the actor Adolphe Menjou – whose last major role would be in Stanley Kubrick's *Paths of Glory*. She picked up a pencil and began a letter to Laura to tell her the big news: 'Edmund has asked me to marry him when I return to England.'

With matters thus settled, Sophia and Nora took Lorraine to the Toeg family bosom and she moved into their L.A. apartment. And now began the lengthy consideration of where she and Edmund might live – the list of possibilities included the United States, Mexico and Italy. As she mulled them over, Lorraine felt that her dreams were coming true: 'Never did think a few years ago that I would be going to live in such countries,' she wrote to Laura.

She had her heart set on a Paris wedding and by early October Lorraine and Edmund were in the French capital, observing the decencies by sleeping under different roofs. Lorraine was sharing a room with Hazel Jones in a hotel near the *Opéra Comique*, where they went to see performances of the *Tales of Hoffman* and *Die*

Rosenkavalier. The trio socialised with a Shanghailander family called the Comptons, who were old friends of the Toegs—a connection that would continue on for decades.

The Comptons were 'awfully wealthy' and lived in luxury hotels—but the wealth of the Toegs was a matter of growing concern, as the liquidation of the family assets in Shanghai became more and more problematic. If the family mansion on Yu Yuen Road could be sold in exchange for the Kuomintang's new gold-backed currency, then Edmund's share would amount to a considerable sum—but he would not be allowed to take the money out of the country. So in order to benefit, he and Lorraine would have to live in China, and they briefly considered moving to Beijing. But as Lorraine pointed out to Laura, 'China could collapse to the Communists anytime'—and 'anytime' came a lot sooner than most expected. Just as Lorraine was writing this letter, the Red Army was crushing its Kuomintang opponent at the Battle of Jinzhou, which allowed the Communists to break out into the North China Plain. Four months later, the Red Army took Beijing.

On 9 November, Edmund and Lorraine's forthcoming marriage was reported in her old paper, the Sydney *Sun*, under the headline 'Sydney Girl to wed in Paris'—in fact the 'Girl' was actually 38, and even nominally she was 34. In an interview with the *Sun*'s Paris stringer, Lorraine had been unable to resist the opportunity to give herself a makeover and claimed that she had spent the last year working for the Ministry of Defence in London; back in Australia, the clipping went on Lorraine's security file. But as it happened, the Sydney Girl was *not* to wed in Paris. A hitch arose, so the couple re-crossed the Channel and were finally married in the registry office at Caxton Hall in Westminster. This was the society venue for secular marriage ceremonies in London—in the coming years, both Elizabeth

Taylor and Joan Collins would also get married there.

It was the culmination not just of Lorraine's own ambition, but of her mother Laura's as well. The entire family was now respectable.

II

'THERE I WAS, A MARRIED WOMAN ...'

a flutter even with a large "F"

Mrs Lorraine Toeg

LORRAINE MARRIED Edmund because she wanted a husband, and because he was wealthy, well-connected and available. Edmund married Lorraine because he wanted someone to look after him, and because she was familiar with his quirks. These calculations aside, there were real bonds of affection between them. And at this stage, the fourteen-year age gap between them seemed to matter less in their relationship than it had when they first met in Shanghai, or later, when Edmund had reached his seventies.

Days after their marriage in London, they were back in a freezing Paris. In the three weeks they spent there, Lorraine fired off a volley of letters to Laura and her sister Margaret. Besides Paris fashions, a major topic was the collapse of the Kuomintang's fortunes in mainland China and, consequently, of the hopes of getting the Toeg family money out of Shanghai. An offer had been made for the family mansion; it was only a fraction of the asking price but the buyer was offering to pay in U.S. dollars. Edmund was so sure of the sale that he 'had already picked out our car and I was to have a mink coat'. But then the

Kuomintang's military position in North China disintegrated and the offer was withdrawn.

By mid-December the couple were in Nice. The Riviera's dramatic coastline and eucalyptus trees reminded Lorraine of Sydney's northern beaches where she had swum as a teenager, and the South of France moved to the top of their list of possible places to live.

Lorraine was a social chameleon, adept at taking on the colouring of her surroundings and now, snug in her new-found status as the wife of a wealthy man, she embraced Edmund's 'old school' class prejudices. In one letter to Laura she wrote:

> *There is a change in the type of English visitor here these days, the men look like waiters or stewards and racing touts, with their wives expensively turned out in Parisian style, but we often are amused when we hear them speak, in a cockney or common type of voice.*

For a long time Lorraine had felt excluded; now, having finally made it inside the charmed circle of good society, it was her turn to do the excluding. It was a privilege she would exercise frequently and while it was a reaction to her previous insecurity, it still seems like an overreaction. At times, like a grotesque overreaction.

In January 1949, Lorraine paid a quick visit to Britain, to obtain a passport in her married name. She travelled down to *Conygar* to see Emily and caught up with Hazel Jones in London. Then, passing through Paris on her way back, she had a sensational brief encounter with Emilio Pucci, Marchese di Barsento, founder of the Pucci fashion house.

There was a Shanghai connection. Pucci had visited the city in the early 1930s, when he had met Mussolini's daughter Edda and her husband Galeazzo Ciano, who was then serving as the Italian Consul General. As Ciano rose to become Italian Foreign Minister, Pucci remained one of the power couple's circle. Then in 1944, when Ciano was executed by the Nazis for rebelling against Mussolini, Pucci helped Edda escape from Italy into Switzerland. For this he had been arrested and tortured by the Gestapo.

When Lorraine came across him, Pucci had just embarked on his career as a fashion designer. They met on the train from London to Paris, and when she missed her onward connection to Nice, she fell in with Pucci's suggestion to stay in his luxury hotel. As she told Emily:

> *I was so happy, there I was a married woman, quite correct for me to be having a flutter even with a large "F", I had nice clothes, independent as far as money was concerned, and a handsome man of the world ... somehow his line of talk and lovemaking was so well known, I knew exactly what would happen next – Italians do stick to the same pattern. He sent off a telegram to Edmund saying I'd arrive in a few days' time, yes, even the same thoughtfulness for Edmund that my other Italians had (remember Luigi bought a hat for Ed from Hongkong once.) When I returned Ed was at station with a bouquet of flowers to meet me, I told him about Emilio, he was quite pleased and said I was clever to grab myself a Marquis. He is snobbish himself at times.*

She also wrote to her sister Margaret about her adventure, and these letters to her closest confidantes were a declaration that her marriage to Edmund was largely devoid of conventional sexual intimacy—and that he accepted her looking elsewhere for it. Lorraine told Emily: 'He says he doesn't mind me having boyfriends if it makes me happy, as he knows he can never give me any sex life'.

When Emily enquired later about the subject, Lorraine replied that she was 'very fed up with his performance'. Six months into their marriage, they had had sex just once; 'But I have been promised a "party" (*code for sex*) tomorrow night, that will be after golf, as Ed is frightened of weakening himself if he indulges before the game'. Talking things over, Lorraine suggested to Edmund that his aversion to intercourse had come about because

> *... he had been educated sexually by "Down the Line" girls* (the prostitutes of Kiangse Road), *who were only after his money, and were keeping themselves to have a good time with their boyfriends and naturally encouraged all sorts of perversions, such as handplaying and getting him worked up by flagellations and such.*

And when she asked him whether he had ever enjoyed sex outside prostitution, Edmund had replied:

> *"I'm not good-looking or the romantic type, so how could I ever attract a girl, I could only go "down the Line" and pay for my fun". Mickey, I felt so touched by him telling me this ... so now I always tell him he is handsome and so attractive and that he is just my type. I think he needs bolstering up all the time, as he has suffered from such an inferior complex all his life and it accounts for so many of his actions.*

Things were sunnier outside the bedroom. Lorraine and Edmund blended right in with the cosmopolitan *rentier* society gathered along the Riviera. Lorraine revelled in the milieu, admiring the Latin American plutocrats who thronged the beaches: 'so rich and sleek, their women so attractive too'. In May, Cannes became the centre of world attention when Prince Ali Khan, of the Nizari Ismaili sect of Shia Islam, married Rita Hayworth there. It was the celebrity wedding of the decade: Hollywood gossip queen Louella Parsons arrived to cover the event and Ali Khan punched several news photographers (this was before the term paparazzi had been coined).

Edmund worked at his art, including portraits of Lorraine—both 'draped and undraped'. But an undraped Wunsy was one thing in private, another in public. Her swimming costume, which had been the '*dernier cri* on Sydney beaches' only two years before, now made her feel conspicuously dowdy as all the other women on the beach were wearing 'the French costume'. This was the bikini, which had just made its appearance, and of which she wrote 'no one seems to take the slightest notice as the French girls have such good figures and the beaches are so well behaved, there don't seem to be the equivalent here of the larrikin type'. Lorraine wanted to get a bikini, but the 'old fashioned' Edmund put his foot down: 'He doesn't like the idea of his wife or sisters to wear one'—though that didn't stop him drawing other women who *did* wear them.

The lotus eaters of the Cote D'Azur came from all over the world. Lorraine and Edmund played mahjong with the former Swiss Consul in Shanghai, who lived in Monte Carlo 'in order to avoid taxes, like many other Shanghai people'. Many of these Shanghailanders were living in what journalist Edward Ward called 'a dream world of the past: in a world of foreign domination and international settlements', and they fantasised that their colonial-era privilege could somehow be salvaged.

Lorraine recorded how at first, these people hoped that history could simply be reversed:

> *Some of the ex-China people we meet are all hoping that Mme Chiang Kai-shek will offer back Shanghai to the Europeans again. Roosevelt gave Shanghai back to China immediately after the war against all the advice ... This business would never have happened in Sh'hai if Ex-territorial rights* (the autonomous status of the International Settlement) *had not been abandoned.*

Then some Shanghailanders began to wonder whether the victorious Chinese Communist Party might somehow be persuaded to welcome them back, and this misreading shaded over into actual support for the CCP. In April the British warship *HMS Amethyst* was steaming up the Yangtze River when it became trapped behind Communist lines. One might have expected the loyalist Lorraine to rally to the Royal Navy; instead she joined in condemnation of it: 'We all feel that the *Amethyst* had no right to be in the battle area the time she was hit'.

Meanwhile, the Kuomintang leadership had fled China. T.V. Soong, Lorraine's former customer in Madame Louise's, turned up in Paris, having transferred abroad much of the vast wealth he had acquired over two decades acting as the regime's financier—as she put it, he was 'well upholstered with silver'. And by the end of May 1949, Shanghai itself had fallen into Communist hands. Initially at least, the CCP took pains to ensure an orderly transition and emigre hopes rose again: 'it seems the Communists in China have done a much better job in keeping law and order than the former Govt. ever did', Lorraine wrote. 'Most of the China people we know here have returned to Hongkong' – preparing for what they hoped would be their return to Shanghai.

In the wake of the Pucci flutter, Lorraine had told Emily she was just waiting 'for another Marquis to tumble into my lap'. And now one did – though this time not a marquis, but a marquise.

Edmund played golf all the time, but Lorraine's irritation at being deserted for the links was softened by the elevated social tone of the Biot Club where he played. Other golfers there included the Duke of Windsor, Prince Rainier of Monaco – later to marry Grace Kelly – and the Aga Khan, Rita Hayworth's new father-in-law.

Edmund's golfing partner was an Italian called Pellegrini, who was the lover of the Marquise de Castellane. So the Marquise was like Lorraine, a golf widow, and soon the two women discovered they had other things in common. As Lorraine explained to Emily

> *Pellegrini partners Ed and they've become good friends so I've often spent a few nights in her villa, and she even turned out Pellegrini from her double bed so I can sleep with her. Then to make things complicated he goes and makes passes at me in the kitchen ...*

This is the only outright reference to a lesbian encounter in Lorraine's surviving correspondence, but it's clear from the tone that it would not have come as a surprise to Emily. And the Marquise was worth bragging about, a trophy catch, her mother having been heiress to a Philadelphia newspaper fortune and her father a distinguished French diplomat. Moreover, the Marquise's recently deceased husband had been the son of the fabulous *belle epoque* influencer Paul Ernest Boniface de Castellane, a model for the character Saint-Loup in Proust's *À la recherche du temps perdu.*

Lorraine's newly empowered snobbery had a strong sexual streak, and the Riviera offered her ample scope to indulge it. And why not? Aristocrats were plentiful and sexual big game hunting was a favoured sport among their social inferiors—like the author Patrick Leigh Fermor, memorably described by Somerset Maugham as 'a middle-class gigolo for upper-class women'. That summer, Lorraine and the Marquise were much in each other's company. She had a car, 'a wonderful cook and servants' and was a friend of Wallis Simpson. This last connection made the Marquise a source of sensational gossip, such as the news that, during her recent visit to Europe, Princess Margaret had made a private call on the Duke and Duchess of Windsor at their Paris flat.

It was all a long way from *Gidgee.*

And yet, even though Lorraine and Edmund were moving in the best circles, their worries about being accepted never quite left them. When the question of them visiting Lorraine's family came up, they were confronted by the immigration policy known as 'White Australia'. On Edmund's passport, his father was described as 'non-British', which implied 'non-white', and he worried that as a result he might be refused entry to Australia. As Lorraine wrote to Laura:

> *Ed is very sensitive about all this, and would simply love to visit Australia, but wonders if there would be any embarrassing trouble when landing, even on a visit ... Anyhow he looks as British as anything and looks no darker than any brunette in Australia, in fact not as dark as Italians or Greeks. I was quite surprised to find he was considered an Oriental ...*

For her part Lorraine had long felt at a disadvantage in her relationship with Edmund's sister Nora. But now came news from Los Angeles which, she felt, put her in a stronger position.

Among the 'China Whites' who had fetched up in California was the Scotsman Dan Cormie, who between the wars had served in the Shanghai Municipal Police. At that time, as a member of the lower orders, Cormie had been a target of the disdain that wealthy Shanghailanders like Dodie Beatty and the Toegs displayed towards their social inferiors. But now it turned out that Nora was marrying the working class Scotsman even though – as Lorraine gleefully pointed out to Emily – during his time as a policeman, Cormie had kept Chinese mistresses, and had even brought his Eurasian daughter with him in America.

The balance of respectability between the sisters-in-law had evened up.

With the end of their honeymoon approaching, Lorraine prodded Edmund into taking a trip to Italy, and over a month they drove to Rome and back along roads flanked by war-damaged buildings. The interlude rekindled Lorraine's affection for Italians, who struck her as modest and industrious in comparison with the French. But by mid-November they were back in London, having made up their minds that they would live in England.

In a letter to Laura, Lorraine reflected on her first year of marriage. Edmund was 'a wonderful husband' she cooed, 'so considerate, and we say that neither of us could have married anyone else, but for the war years we really would have married sooner.' Writing to Emily, she sounded more like a wife: 'He misses the racing and his damn cricket and football. Those sports bore me completely. If I want trips abroad I can see I will have to take a job to earn the extra money. Isn't he pigheaded.'

She had always wanted to be normal. Now she was.

III

THE BRIGHT FACADES OF TRADITION

One falls automatically into one's class

Lorraine Toeg

RETURNING TO ENGLAND, Lorraine crossed a watershed in her life. In the previous two decades she had moved home more than twenty times, but once settled in London she would stay put in the same house until she returned to Australia in 1985. London became her world, Europe her horizon, and she never went back to China. And from now on, the major source for Lorraine's life becomes her regular fortnightly letter to Laura, written on blue Royal Mail aerogram forms.

In one of these, Lorraine said, 'I think I must have inherited this letter writing from you – at least in receiving & the obligation of answering letters – It is certainly a 'hangover' of the Victorian Age – Queen Victoria herself was a terrific letter writer'. It's a comment that resonates well beyond their correspondence: Laura was very much a product of the Late Victorian Age – and the apple never falls very far from the tree.

Lorraine's letters to Emily in the period 1944 to 1946, for all their candour, were written with the purpose of persuading her best friend that she had changed, improved – reformed. In the same way, her letters to Laura also have a theme, but a different one: respectability. She trumpets her acceptance in society and it's clear that Laura shared vicariously in her daughter's success. This celebration of Lorraine's social ascent helped both to bury ever deeper the anxiety and shame that they had experienced as younger women.

The London to which Edmund and Lorraine returned was a wreck, scarred by wartime bombing and heavily polluted. When he arrived in the city a year later, the novelist George Johnston found it

> *... a leaden grey place, and the faces in the queues are grey and docile: there are queues for buses, for ration books, for cod-liver oil and orange juice, they even queue sometimes because there is a queue and they wonder hopefully what is at the end of it. They queue patiently to take their turn to watch men clearing away bomb debris ... Behind the gay fashionable streets and the bright facades of tradition the heavy grey wilderness is gigantic and brooding ...*

There was no escaping grey, the mark of the city's dependence on coal, which left everything covered in soot and which was soon to kill thousands of people in the event called the Great Smog. The ruins were equally hard to ignore: Edmund's cousin Victor Toeg lived in a house in St John's Wood which was 'surrounded by burnt out shells of houses and gardens littered with glass & marble'. After scouting this unpromising cityscape for some months, in June 1950 Lorraine and Edmund picked out their future home, 15 Rutland Mews, Knightsbridge, though not without misgivings: 'Some of the large homes in the neighbourhood are burnt out shells & it made us rather depressed the first time we went into our Mews'.

In compensation, London offered a readymade circle of friends and acquaintances. Having lived in Shanghai, Edmund and Lorraine belonged to a club whose members popped up everywhere. While they were looking around for a home they had taken a flat in Earls Court; their neighbour, a retired colonel, turned out to have served in Shanghai. When they moved into Rutland Mews, they found that a neighbour there had been a bank manager in the International Settlement. Then in July, Edmund's mother Sophia and his sister Dora arrived to settle in England, the scene of the family's Edwardian glory days. As Lorraine explained to Laura, 'we really know so many people here that our spare time is always spent with others'.

Sport, which had previously tied Edmund to the Shanghailander elite, now became his bridge to a new life in London. Soon he was 'going to Lords quite a bit with his old Sh'hai cronies', who included Geoffrey Fitzgerald, his shooting companion on the *Nora*. Fitzgerald hosted a welcome party for the couple at which the guests were 'old Sh'hai friends' and where the talk was of 'horsey days of Paper Hunts'. Other friends included the journalist Edward Ward and Lionel Sackville-West. Sackville-West had worked in Shanghai for Jardine Matheson, one of the leading British firms trading with China, and he would soon inherit one of the grandest of English country homes, Knole in Kent.

By happy chance Fitzgerald, Ward and Sackville-West were all aristocrats, and if London was in ruins the British class system remained intact. The Shanghai-born novelist J.G. Ballard discovered this when after the war he arrived in England for the first time. Reared amongst the vivid colours and contrasts of China, Ballard found it hard to adjust to a monochrome England—'a small grey country where the sun rarely rose above the rooftops'—and even more difficult to adapt to its opaque society: 'a labyrinth of class and caste forever enlarging itself from within'.

But Lorraine plunged confidently into this labyrinth, following her conviction that 'one falls automatically into one's class'. Explaining the hierarchy to Laura, she placed herself and Edmund among the 'comfortable middle class', who lived off investment income. As such, they ranked distinctly above the 'lower middle class', who were 'rather hard to mix with as they are frightened of losing the standing they have'—as well they might be, because only the thinnest of lines separated them from the working class. And the working class were not just 'loutish', but 'tiring' and 'depressing' as well; nevertheless they had one redeeming feature: they 'loved the Upper Classes', which was topped by a hereditary aristocracy who were 'a race apart'. Lorraine positively drooled over 'the handsome smooth-skinned Guards officers' who lived in Knightsbridge.

To her, this hierarchy was both natural and desirable, and within it she found the secure social position she craved. So it's not surprising that when it came to politics she stood firmly on the right, and with just the occasional liberal wobble, her attachment to the Tories would last the whole of her life in England.

Among their Shanghailander circle, the positive view of the new Peoples Republic of China persisted—at least in the short term. The impression was that 'so far (*the Communists*) are all idealists working for the benefit of people & to put China economically on her feet'.

But the new rulers of China showed little indulgence towards the likes of Sir Victor Sassoon. Now settled in the tax haven of the Bahamas, Sassoon reported to Edmund that the Communist authorities had levied punitive taxes on his properties in Shanghai. He had given up any hope of selling of these, but he couldn't just ignore their demands, because the authorities were holding his manager hostage. The Communists had also issued the Toegs with a hefty tax bill on their family property, but they had left no hostages behind and just refused to pay.

As the loss of their assets in Shanghai sank in, it became clear that the Toeg fortune had been sadly diminished. Not all the family had adjusted to the new circumstances: Mrs Toeg kept up her *belle epoque* habits of ordering champagne by the case and employing a chauffeur, horrifying Lorraine. She confided to Emily that 'Ed is acting tightly & says we have to go easy'.

Now in his mid-fifties, Edmund was too old to find a place in the City of London. He dabbled in the stock exchange but only in small amounts – a £30 profit in a month was a good result, and half of that went in tax. Rather, he planned to live off his annuity and 'make a bit here & there with his Art'. Lorraine saw lean times ahead, but took comfort in the thought that 'we will be in same boat as all our friends & others of the middle classes'.

But in fact, theirs was a privileged situation. Readers of *Empire Made Me*, Robert Bickers' book about colonial Shanghai, will be struck by the post-war disparity in fortunes between on the one hand the Toegs, their relatives and friends, and the underclass of British colonial society on the other. Many of what Bickers' called these 'other ranks' of colonial society had emerged from Japanese internment camps into penury. Many emigrated to places like Hong Kong, New Zealand, Canada, what was then Rhodesia, or the Philippines. A number wound up in Australia; in the mid-1950s, Sydney would boast a 'Shanghai Police Association'. But despite some golden memories, their lives in Shanghai had brought them little material benefit. In contrast, many of the wealthy Shanghailanders effortlessly resumed their places in the Establishment or retired to some tax haven.

From the tone of her early London letters to Laura, it would be easy to dismiss Lorraine in these years as a social alpinist, and there would be some grounds for such a judgement. But alongside her snobbery, her intellectual curiosity was leading her on to a new circle of friends outside Edmund's moneyed and sporting connections, including artists, actors, writers, and composers. Some of them were neighbours, among them the South Australian actor Keith Michell. The two got on well, and for some years Lorraine regularly went to see him perform at the theatre.

At the end of 1950, Jardine Matheson hosted a grand party in the Dorchester Hotel. The occasion was to welcome home Tony Keswick, one of the company's senior managers, who together with his wife had been being held hostage in Shanghai. Among the guests were the Fitzgeralds, the journalist Christopher Chancellor—who had been the Reuters bureau chief in Shanghai in the 1930s—and several former British ambassadors to China. Lorraine was delighted to find Edmund was 'so popular' in this exclusive circle.

There would be many such functions in the future, but their apogee would be *the* society wedding of 1953, at which fashion model Jane McNeill married the Earl of Dalkeith. Edmund and Lorraine were invited because of his friendship with the bride's father, a lawyer who had practiced in Shanghai before the war. The groom was the largest private landowner in the U.K. and was close to the Royal Family—very close to Princess Margaret, whom at one point he had been expected to marry—and the British elite mustered strong for the wedding. Held in Edinburgh's St Giles Cathedral, it was attended by the Queen, the Duke of Edinburgh, Princess Margaret, other members of the Royal Family, dukes, duchesses and lesser aristocracy galore. Another guest was General Telfer-Smollett, whose heroic rescue of a Chinese woman during the Battle of Shanghai had been witnessed by Norman Alley.

And then there was Mr and Mrs Edmund Toeg. It was Lorraine's apotheosis: as she emerged at the cathedral entrance from a hired limousine, clad in a velvet suit, mauve helmet hat and 'all my jewels', the gathered crowd cheered and children waved flags—Edmund explained gallantly that she must have been taken for an actress. Inside, the Royal Party passed close enough for Lorraine to remark on the Queen's 'lovely complexion'.

The ghost of Johnny Jean had finally been laid to rest.

There was a London sequel to the McNeill wedding. The bride's aunt, the Countess of Jersey, organised a charity show, a farce called *Lord & Lady Algy* with real lords among the actors and the proceeds going to benefit underprivileged children. Again, the Toegs were invited, and Lorraine wore a new ballet length evening dress with a fur cape and 'all her jewels'. Sir Victor Sassoon, visiting from Nassau, was among the audience and as Lorraine enthused: 'Never have I seen so many beautiful women & wonderful dresses & bejewelled'—and she was one of them. It was all quite enchanting even though, as Edmund pointed out, the charitable purpose of the event had been rendered unnecessary by the advent of the welfare state, as there were no longer any underprivileged children. Lorraine agreed: 'The working class child is so spoilt now'.

Sometimes Lorraine's attitudes can bring you up with a jolt. Another, less abrupt, example was a devotion to the monarchy which was almost religious in its intensity. She had been in London for the Coronation of George VI, and she was in London when he died in February 1952. The account she sent Laura makes his death seem almost like a cosmic event.

It seemed to her like one of those moments when time slows right down, when people go over the smallest detail again and again. 'What a terrible shock we all had yesterday hearing of the King's Death,' her account begins. 'A sort of gloom hung over everything'.

Rumours were circulating ahead of the official announcement, and she describes the lengths to which she and Edmund went to confirm the news, the crowds gathering in the streets and the government's fear that the arrival of the new Queen in London might trigger hysterical crushes among crowds. Her reverence for the monarch would persist; when, some years later, Lorraine's brother Peter and his wife were presented to the Queen during a Royal Visit to Australia, Lorraine said she 'could have wept with joy'. It was more than a figure of speech.

And it was a brush with royalty that gave Lorraine the opportunity to resume contact with her old lover, Tokugawa Iemasa. In 1953 the Japanese Crown Prince Akihito travelled to London to attend the coronation of Queen Elizabeth—we recall that his mother, the Empress Kojun, was the niece of Tokugawa's wife. Edmund and Lorraine attended a gala dinner in the Crown Prince's honour, and Lorraine took the occasion as an opportunity to re-open communication: 'I wrote to Prince Tokugawa about the dinner for the Crown Prince,' she told Laura. He was so happy to hear from me & said he took no time in going to Toyoko's house & showing her my letter ...'.

Lorraine's marriage to Edmund had been crowned with triumphs like the McNeill wedding. She had not just wiped her slate clean, she had arrived on the very threshold of elite British society. She was now unimpeachably respectable, and this was the message when she returned to home to Australia for a visit in November 1953. Her arrival in Sydney was reported by the *Sun*, to whom she described herself—just to set the record absolutely straight—as 'the wife of an English stockbroker whom she met while holidaying in Shanghai before the war'.

IV

Document J

Oh what is in Document J ...
Everyone's asking today.
There ain't no knowin'
Says Justice Owen
Just what is in Document J ...
Oh what is in Document J ...
ASIO says it's OK
To have the Feds
Look under our beds
For the Commies in Document J ...
Sydney pub song, 1954

London's bombed cityscape was not only a reminder of the last war, but a portent of the next. It was a danger Lorraine was acutely aware of; when the Soviet Union conducted an atomic test, she said she feared 'Russia is likely to bomb cities without any warning of war.'

It's difficult now to conceive of just how imminent that threat then felt. In Britain, the government calculated that as much as one-third of the population would perish in a Soviet nuclear attack. People believed that war could break out at any moment: one night, drinking in his favourite London pub, George Johnston noticed how 'people in nine different groups were talking about the possibility of World War III'. Lorraine's years in London would be punctuated by crises such as the building of the Berlin Wall, the Cuban Missile Crisis and the Yom Kippur War, any one of which might have escalated into a nuclear conflict. And this sense of the imminence of a cataclysm was amplified by the threat of espionage, because unlike the menace of Axis spies during the Second World War—which (with hindsight) had proved to be overstated—Soviet intelligence posed an acute danger to the West.

Just as Lorraine and Edmund were settling down in London, the city was transfixed by one the first major espionage scandals of the Cold War, as the German/British scientist Klaus Fuchs was convicted at the Old Bailey for having passed nuclear secrets to Moscow. It was a time of suspicion and fear, a time of 'Commo agents and Commo spies lurking under every desk and table', as Johnston put it. People worried that even trusted friends might not be what they seemed, and Lorraine shared in the widespread paranoia. In the wake of the Fuchs trial, she wrote to Laura to warn her against a family friend in Australia: like Fuchs, the man was a scientist and, Lorraine was certain, a covert communist.

It was perhaps incongruous that the sleepy backwater of Canberra should have been the scene of a major Cold War intelligence scandal, but so it was. This came about because over the previous decades, Australia had been the recipient of a great deal of top secret British and American information, but had failed to protect it. Towards the end of World War II, a group of communist sympathisers in the Sydney office of Herbert 'Doc' Evatt, the then Minister for External Affairs, had begun hoovering up classified materials and passing them to the Soviet

Embassy. They belonged to a network headed by Communist Party of Australia (CPA) functionary Walter Clayton, who served as its link to Soviet intelligence officers. And Rupert Lockwood, Lorraine's old sparring partner, was Clayton's close contact and regular drinking companion.

Soon the group's activities spread to the Department of External Affairs in Canberra, where one of its members was the diplomat Jim Hill. Meanwhile, a window into the activities of Soviet intelligence worldwide had been opened by the American VENONA program, which had begun to decode some of the cable traffic between Moscow and its intelligence stations abroad. Slowly, VENONA began to expose some of the Soviet spies in the West, and to deal with the threat the Australian government created a new body, the Australian Security Intelligence Organisation (ASIO), to take over counter intelligence functions from the patently ineffective Commonwealth Investigation Service (CIS), the new name for the old CIB on whose behalf Lorraine had spied on Lockwood.

For his part, Lockwood spent most of the 1940s in Sydney working for the communist newspaper the *Tribune*, before travelling to London in 1948, where he spent a year as the CPA's representative in Britain. Then in 1950 Lockwood was back in Europe and passing through London when an incident occurred which, according to historian John Fahey, unequivocally demonstrates that he was an active communist agent.

Jim Hill was working in the Australian High Commission in London—where Lorraine went regularly to read the *Australian Women's Weekly*—when he was grilled by a security official who, prompted by VENONA revelations, showed a hostile and alarmingly detailed interest in his activities. Panic-stricken, Hill convened an immediate meeting of his communist contacts in London. Summoned to the meeting, Lockwood was sent racing back to Sydney to warn Clayton that his operation had somehow been exposed.

This was a setback for the CPA network. Nevertheless Lockwood continued to make himself useful to the Soviets and during a May 1953 visit to their embassy in Canberra, he typed out the 37-page memorandum that would become known as Document J. An attack on prominent political and business figures, this is one of only a handful of documents that can be said to have changed the course of Australian history, and it featured Lorraine as the inept tool of an inept secret police. Then in April 1954, ASIO engineered the defection of the intelligence officer Vladimir Petrov, who brought with him a satchel of material—including Lockwood's memorandum.

Petrov's defection came as a godsend for the conservative government of Robert Menzies. For some years the legal status of the CPA had been a political football; Menzies had previously tried to outlaw the party but had been defeated by a public campaign headed by the opposition Labor Party, which was now led by 'Doc' Evatt. Menzies hammered away at Evatt and Labor for being soft on the communist menace, but overall the Labor Party was doing well in the polls, and was considered well placed to win the next election.

Petrov's defection caused a sensation. When he defected he had left his wife Evdokia, also an intelligence officer, behind; she was frogmarched onto a plane bound for Russia, only to be dramatically rescued, snatched from the arms of Soviet goons during a refuelling stop in Darwin. Public concern about the communist threat rose to new heights and, ten days after Petrov's defection, the Menzies government established a Royal Commission on Espionage. It was headed by Justice Owen—he who was celebrated in the pub song quoted at the head of this chapter—and the Counsel Assisting (the senior lawyer for the

Government) was Victor Windeyer, who during the war had been the commanding officer of Lorraine's brother John Murray. Soon Owen and Windeyer were poring over Lockwood's Document J.

Later it would be said that when writing Document J, Lockwood was fired up on Russian brandy; if so, this might help explain why his memorandum was so full of venomous slander. In it, Lockwood relates how in wartime Sydney he had met

> *... a very beautiful girl named Lorraine Murray who had been living in Japan with Prince Tokugawa, member of the old feudal shogun family. She left Japan in some kind of disgrace. Dr Peter Russo, former Professor at the Tokio Imperial University, reported that she had contracted syphilis ... Lorraine Murray was under the influence of the Security Police, and worked for them, but she was a remarkably stupid girl.*

There's no evidence, not even any other suggestion, that Lorraine ever contracted syphilis. It's just as likely that this was a smear, either originating in Shanghai where Russo might have heard it, or made up by Russo, or invented by Lockwood himself. It's the sort of revenge slander that men spread about women who reject them, and Lorraine may well have rejected Russo—and Lockwood too.

Document J then went on to say that Lorraine: 'was asked by D.A. Alexander to spy on R. Lockwood (*Lockwood was referring to himself in the third person*) ... Murray promptly told Lockwood that Alexander had asked her to do this ...'

The reason why Document J mentioned Lorraine in the first place was because Lockwood was reaching back into the early

1940s to set the stage for his pet conspiracy theory. This was that, prior to the outbreak of the Pacific War, the Japanese had recruited a network of collaborators from among the highest levels of the Australian establishment, traitors who were prepared to serve as quislings in the event of a Japanese conquest. And that, a decade later, many of these alleged traitors remained in positions of influence, such as Sir Percy Spender, Canberra's long serving Ambassador to the United States. So as a target of Lockwood's malign libels, Lorraine was in good company, alongside a former Governor General, other senior politicians, artists and journalists.

As Counsel Assisting Victor Windeyer put it, the document threw

> *... a glaring light, both on the methods used by Russians and the depths to which an Australian citizen* (Lockwood) *has sunk to help a foreign power ... In one place a man is alleged to have been an embezzler and to have led a woman, who is named, into degenerate conduct and encouraged her to become a dipsomaniac. Another man had a woman acquaintance whose name is also given and says she had syphilis. Another person is said to have had adulterous intercourse with a woman on giving her a promise she would be safe if the Japanese came to Australia.*

Windeyer famously described Document J as 'a farrago of facts, falsity and filth' and recommended that the Royal Commission suppress it. But while the document itself remained secret, some of its content began to leak into the public sphere.

The reason why Document J created such mayhem was not so much because of its claims, noxious though those were, but because of the political context. Soon after the Royal Commission was established, Menzies called an election at which the conservatives were re-elected by the narrowest of margins. It was widely judged that the Petrov Affair, by heightening the perception that Labor and Evatt were unwilling and unable to confront the rampant Soviet and communist menace, had helped the government scrape back into office.

But the damage to Labor didn't stop there. Evatt unwisely made Document J the focus of his attack on the Government's handling of the Petrov case, a tactic which backfired. Evatt's argument was that Document J was a forgery and Lockwood was not its author. But in fact Lockwood *was* the author, as he effectively admitted. The Opposition Leader emerged from the Royal Commission discredited, and his loss of credibility was a contributing factor to the Labor Party's subsequent split over its policy towards communism. And as a result of the split, Australia would remain under conservative rule for more than two decades.

Lockwood's response to the emergence of Document J was, in the words of historian Robert Manne, one of 'defiance and bravado'. As we have noted, Document J was not released to the public, and this enabled Lockwood to argue that while it sounded like something he might have written, he couldn't be sure. So he released a new document entitled 'What is in Document J', in which he repeated many of his claims – but in a sanitised form, to reduce the risk of being sued. This new pamphlet was soon being passed around among politicians, journalists and union officials, and in this way many of the claims in his original memorandum became common currency.

In this new pamphlet Lockwood repeated the story of his relationship with Lorraine. This time he didn't name her but he gave her a good airing as a 'shady lady … beautiful, irresponsible, vicious and slanderous'. But one name Lockwood did rename was that of Lorraine's handler Desmond Alexander, and he lampooned him as a sinister and incompetent buffoon.

The creation of ASIO had relegated Alexander's organisation, the Commonwealth Investigation Service, to the sidelines, and so it and he had nothing directly to do with the Petrov Affair. But when he was ridiculed by Lockwood, Alexander reacted strongly. He consulted a lawyer about suing for libel and he complained to his head office in Canberra that he was being kept in the dark about developments at the Royal Commission. Then the press—including the notorious scandal sheet the *Truth*—began to sniff around. Alexander began to worry about how his wife would react when the news about his relationship with the 'beautiful, irresponsible shady lady' appeared in the *Truth*.

While all this was going on, the 'shady lady' herself was watching events from the other side of the world, in London. And it's now that we learn, somewhat surprisingly, that for the past decade Lorraine had kept in touch with her old wartime colleagues in the CIB, including Alexander. Three letters from her to Alexander concerning the Petrov Affair survive.

The first shows that she and he were old friends:

> *Dear Alex, Thank you so much for the nice card I received from your wife and self for Christmas last … Such interesting news these days about the Petrov case and I read with interest the news of our old friend Mr Lockwood. I had an idea his name would turn up some day when I read of Petrov seeking sanctuary in Australia. You must be very busy in connection with this case.*

It was signed 'Johnnie', her work name at Louise's brothel—

leaving us to wonder if Alexander knew the origins of the nickname.

This was a fishing expedition; Lorraine could not have known that she was named in Document J, because it had been suppressed. But then Alexander sent her a copy of Lockwood's new pamphlet 'What is in Document J', in which she *was* recognisable as the 'shady lady'. And when she read Lockwood's comment that when he knew her in wartime Sydney, Lorraine had 'still retained such trinkets from the past as a sable coat', she disdainfully pointed out that like so much else of what he wrote, this was untrue: the coat was 'not sable, only dyed squirrel!'

Her third letter to Alexander was signed 'Lorraine Toeg', and the more formal tone was appropriate because now she was writing on business: to ask that Tokugawa Iemasa's name be kept out of the scandal.

> *If Document J is going to be published in its entirety, could you see that Prince Tokugawa's name is left out. He is an old man of over seventy – has always been pro-British & educated in the UK & a friend of the Duke of Windsor's. His family suffered during the war for his sentiments & like many of the aristocracy were not wishing for the army to make war.*

Lorraine argued that if the Tokugawa name were to be dragged into the limelight, then it could harm Australia's relations with Japan at the very time when the powerful Japanese Communist Party was looking to detach Japan from the Western Cold War alliance. She had at least a point, but in assuming Alexander could influence matters she was wildly overestimating both his capacity and that of his much-diminished Commonwealth Investigation Service. Alexander's response was a patronising note on the file which brings to an end Lorraine's walk-on role in the Petrov Affair.

Nevertheless their correspondence leaves us wondering about the nature of Lorraine's extended relationship with Alexander and Australian counter-intelligence authorities. Not only had she stayed in touch with him over the past decade, she told him how during her recent visit to Sydney she had dropped in to see 'Mr Barnwell in his office'. Alexander's colleague Bill Barnwell was an old security hand who had worked in Sydney since at least the mid-1930s; the fact that Lorraine could just walk into the CIS office and start chatting to an old friend suggests that she was more than just one of many anonymous wartime informants. For how long did she remain active on their behalf? We don't know.

But the most revealing aspect of Lorraine's letters to Alexander is her parade of snobbery. To her old wartime handler, she emphasised just how far behind she had left Australia ...

> *Leading such a totally different life in London, and rather a social life ... my husband is in contact with members of the House of Lords & is friends of a former British Ambassador to Japan. We are both invited to parties at various embassies ... In September I will fly to Cyprus for a few weeks holiday of swimming and sunbathing which I adore and the South of France is so tripperish* (overrun with working class tourists) *these days. I am tired of Italy ...'*

Nor was her rise confined to the secular world; she told Alexander how she and Edmund had had their registry office marriage blessed in the Farm Street Jesuit Church in Mayfair—'where the Embassy people go'.

The message was clear. When Alexander had recruited her

as an informant in wartime Sydney, she had been a former bar hostess who couldn't even get a job as a shop assistant. Now, she was hobnobbing with aristocrats and ambassadors, being blessed by high society Jesuits and flying off on Mediterranean holidays—in an era when this was the acme of luxury and sophistication. Alexander and Barnwell had seen her at her lowest point; now she was at her best, and she wanted them to know it.

V

'You never had it so good'

One slow descent into respectability

Mandy Rice-Davies

In March 1955, Lorraine's mother-in-law, Sophia Toeg, died. The funeral service was held at the London house of Victor Toeg, Edmund read the Kaddish and, setting the seal of acceptance on Lorraine, Nora and Dora asked her to be the hostess at the gathering. Now she was definitely one of the family—sometimes, in the years ahead, more than she wanted to be.

This was the chronological midpoint of Lorraine's life. The second half of her story—like those of many people—would prove less eventful than the first. There is certainly less to write about, not least because the source material dries up. But to Lorraine, it was in many ways a more fulfilling existence, during which her time as a sex worker, which had so haunted her, would fall into a broader perspective as a small part of a long and varied life.

By the mid-1950s, Britain was changing: Austerity was over and the country was enjoying the economic boom that would prompt Prime Minister Harold Macmillan to tell the British people that 'you never had it so good'. Partly, the change was technological. It was a red letter day when, on her 46th birthday, Lorraine's family in Australia were able to make a telephone call direct to Rutland Mews without having to book it in advance. But British society was changing, too; as she remarked:

> *... nearly every worker wants his children to get into Grammar School & then to a University & hence many raise their level & marry their opposite on a higher social scale – nearly every charwoman's daughter is a typist or secretary ...*

The effects of change were dire: society hostesses were forced to go without maids and middle-class men to do housework; Lorraine had even seen officers of the ultra-fashionable Guards regiments doing their own household shopping in Knightsbridge. This was a challenge to the hierarchy in which Lorraine had found her place, and she found it unsettling.

Some of her unease stemmed from the awareness that her and Edmund's financial position was not as robust as it might have been. Like other members of the 'comfortable middle class', who had made their pile in what she called 'the good old days of cheap labour', they felt threatened. In the topsy-turvy world of progressive taxation, she noted sourly that the only way to get rich was through a gamble on the odiously proletarian football pools. Immigration was another sign of the changing times, but here there was a silver lining: Lorraine preferred to employ 'West Indian girls' as cleaners because they took lower wages.

From now on, while they would never go in anything like want, the couple's financial horizons started to close in and Edmund began to dip into his hoard of *objets d'art*. During the Toegs' glory days, his father had astutely invested in Dutch old master paintings, some of which had wound up in Rutland Mews—the pick of them was Pieter Codde's *Cavaliers and Ladies*, now in the Rijksmuseum in Amsterdam. Around this time, Edmund sold the Codde and began to exhibit some of the Chinese antiques he had brought from Shanghai.

As he entered his sixties, the age gap between Edmund and Lorraine started to matter more. His comfort zone became more narrowly defined, bounded on the west by Rutland Mews, the east by the City of London, where he traded shares, and the north by Lord's Cricket Ground, where he and his old Shanghai friends gathered in Lord's Tavern. But Lorraine yearned to move out into the country, and throughout the 1960s, a constant topic in her letters are the rural cottages for sale that she discovers, but then fails to persuade Edmund to move to. And if it was hard to shift Edmund within Britain, he flatly refused to travel overseas, though he was happy for Lorraine herself to take annual holidays to places like Italy, Spain and Yugoslavia.

If she had to be stuck in London, then there were worse places to be stuck than Knightsbridge. It was a haunt of celebrities: among the neighbours Lorraine and Edmund came to know over the decades were the movie stars Jack Hawkins, Charlton Heston, and David Niven—one of the photos in Lorraine's cherished album was of Niven holding Sammy, her Boxer dog. Sammy achieved his own social apotheosis when he pissed on the Jaguar belonging to Princess Margaret's father-in-law, who lived nearby.

Lorraine's friendship with Emily flourished. The record of their relationship in the 1950s is sparse, but this was not because the two women had become more distant. In fact, Emily and Charles had moved from Dorset to Little Gaddesden in Hertfordshire, about forty kilometers northwest of London. Living so close to each other, the two women didn't need to stay in touch by letter, and so only a handful survive from this period—given the frankness of their correspondence, a distinct loss. But we know Lorraine remained very close to Emily and her family, particularly when her daughter Carola moved to London later in the decade.

By now the dominant note in Lorraine's memories of Shanghai was nostalgia rather than paranoia. It had been gratifying to be accepted by Edmund's Shanghailander circle, to be invited to grand occasions like the McNeill wedding and to visit the gardens at Sackville-West great estate at Knole. But these people were Edmund's old friends—not hers. Because London was such a global crossroads, Lorraine increasingly came across people whom she herself had known in Shanghai—which meant that they were often friends of Emily's as well. When this happened all the romance and excitement of life at 'good old 1826' Avenue Joffre came flooding back to her.

Luigi Barzini resurfaced. Preparing to go on a journalistic assignment to Hong Kong and Taiwan, he contacted Edmund and Lorraine to ask them if they could put him in touch with people he could interview. He also invited them to stay with him on his estate outside Rome and Lorraine would take up this offer on her Italian holidays. Barzini's book *The Italians*, which would make him famous in the Anglophone world, was published in the early 1960s. When it appeared, Lorraine commented, rather tartly, that 'Luigi always appointed himself as spokesman of his people'.

Among the other old Shanghai friends was the American journalist and author John Gunther, who moved to England in the mid-1950s. It was Gunther's recommendation to a New York publisher which had resulted in Emily being commissioned to write her breakthrough book *The Soong Sisters*. Another was Ake Hartman, whom Emily mentioned in *China to Me* as the man who introduced her to the Japanese journalist Horiguchi Yoshinori, who later became Lorraine's lover. Lorrane bumped into Hartman at a London party and wrote to Emily 'Ake recognized me immediately ... He spoke so much about you & he was dying to see you again'.

In her late forties, a new Lorraine began to emerge—in many ways a more interesting character than any of her previous incarnations. Her work ethic resurfaced: she went back to regular employment; at first in a travel agency and temporary clerical jobs, she then moved into administrative and librarian positions in learned societies, think tanks and professional bodies.

Her interest in the arts deepened. She made friends in the creative community, among them the intersex Italian sculptor Fiore de Henriquez. A veteran of the Italian Resistance, de Henriquez settled in England where she embarked on a remarkably successful and prolific career. From de Henriquez, Edmund commissioned a portrait head of Lorraine, which featured as a table centrepiece for dinner parties at Rutland Mews.

One of Lorraine's more important friends in the coming decades would be the German/Israeli musician, teacher and composer Peter Feuchtwanger. He was a neighbour in Rutland Mews, where he lived with his partner, the Sydney-born painter Michael Garaday. Lorraine attended the premiere of Feuchtwanger's *Variation on an Eastern Folk Tune* in Wigmore Hall.

But it was in her political outlook that the change in Lorraine's attitudes is most obvious. In her letters we now hear less about overprivileged workers and cheap labour, more about social issues and political alternatives. She even (temporarily) shifted her allegiance from the Tories to the Liberal Party (now subsumed into the Liberal Democrats). This, she rationalised, was not so much a desertion of the conservative cause but rather a way of supporting it by wooing voters away from Labour: 'there must be something to offer between Tory & Socialists & many Socialists will vote Liberal, but would not vote Tory'.

This shift partly reflected the influence of Carola Boxer, who had moved to London. Prompted by her youthful enthusiasm, Lorraine began to engage with various issues of the day. Carola took her to meet the Reverend Austen Williams, the Anglican vicar of St Martins-in-the-Fields. A social activist, Williams ministered to a Chinese congregation and set up a soup kitchen for homeless people, where Lorraine would do volunteer work. After the March 1960 Sharpeville massacre in South Africa, Lorraine, again inspired by Carola, began to attend meetings protesting against Apartheid.

But just as her life was taking this turn, the demands of being a member of the Toeg family began to weigh more on her. In early 1958, Edmund had a slight stroke, and late in that year Dora had an accident which left her incapacitated: Lorraine had to step in to help care for her. The health of the Toegs now became a major topic of Lorraine's letters, underlining the fact that after a decade of marriage, the paths of Dee Dee and Wunsy were starting to diverge.

Edmund was all for a quiet life but as she entered her fifties, Lorraine was just getting into her stride, proclaiming to Laura 'one must keep mentally & physically active to survive'. Her life wasn't just active; it was frenetic: among other things she embarked on a comprehensive program of self-education. In one letter she mentions that she just had completed one course, on

English Architecture, and was about to enrol in another: she was tossing up between Spanish Art and Architecture and Russian Language. For her 51st birthday, Edmund gave her a membership of the Italian Cultural Institute, where she attended conversation classes. She had developed an interest in Sephardic Judaism and delved into the history of the Toegs.

So much for intellectual fulfillment, but it's unclear how she satisfied her other needs. In the regrettable absence of her confiding letters to Emily, we lose sight of Lorraine's *vie intime*. It seems unlikely that she derived much sexual satisfaction from her relationship with Edmund. There are some vague hints of how she found her pleasure: she and Peter Feuchtwanger went out socialising to venues like The Rockingham, a gay club in Soho's Archer Street, and to their local The Ennismore Arms, which also had the reputation of being gay-friendly. She went on holiday to Spain with a female couple, and afterwards stayed with them in their village home outside Oxford. On the basis of a few such sparse indications, it seems that Lorraine enjoyed herself in the company of like-minded women.

Lorraine's description of English society under the Macmillan Conservative government gives the impression of an orderly calm. Despite worrying signs that the working class were getting above themselves, the 'comfortable middle classes' were managing to hold their ground. And with the exception of a few liberal enthusiasms such as the anti-Apartheid movement Lorraine, a nostalgic Tory, remained wedded to the Establishment. But just across Hyde Park a drama was unfolding which would come to symbolise the death of the conservative dispensation which was her spiritual home.

Around this time, the society osteopath Stephen Ward had

met Christine Keeler, a seventeen-year-old dancer in a Soho cabaret club: she became his protégé and moved into his mews house. Ward introduced her to his high society friends, including the conservative politician Lord William Astor, and the junior defence minister John Profumo, who was married to the actress Valerie Hobson. In 1961, Keeler had affairs with both Profumo and Yevgeny Ivanov, a Russian spy. Keeler's friend and fellow showgirl Mandy Rice-Davies was part of this circle and the two young women followed the same sort of demimondaine lifestyle that a quarter of a century before, Lorraine had lived in Shanghai.

As long as they remained secret, Keeler's and Rice-Davies' transactional relationships with prominent men were in keeping with the English Establishment's tradition. But when they came out into the open in early 1963, the revelation punctured the bubble of upper class hypocrisy. Rice-Davies nailed it: in court, when told that Astor denied having sex with her, she replied 'He would, wouldn't he?' It was the epitaph for the old order Lorraine so much admired.

Profumo initially told Parliament that there had been no impropriety in his relationship with Keeler, then he was forced to admit he had lied, and he resigned. But the political damage didn't end there: the Profumo Affair helped bring down Prime Minister Macmillan, who resigned in October. French President Charles De Gaulle commented: 'That'll teach the English for trying to behave like Frenchmen'. The Tories lost government the following year.

Lorraine's reaction to the scandal was to rally behind the Conservatives. Shortly after Profumo's resignation, she attended a function organised by the Tory party. The fete was opened by Valerie Profumo, who

> *got a wonderful welcome and many cheers. She said she*

> *thought she should retire from public life owing to all the scandal, but was advised by Young Conservatives to open the fete as previously planned, and when her speech was replied to, they said, she had been a brave wife and mother and people wanted her to feel that all that is now passed and how they admire her etc. ... The* (Profumo) *family have had a marvellous record in setting up Charity trusts and scholarships. Jack* (Profumo) *was educated at Harrow. It is too bad that all this should have happened ...*

Lorraine and Edmund seem to have been personally acquainted with the Profumos and so perhaps it is not surprising that she should have applauded the brave wife and mother, excused the errant 'Jack', and brushed 'all this'—which included Keeler and Rice-Davies—aside.

And yet ... while Lorraine was a generation older than Keeler and Rice-Davies, she had more in common with them that she cared to acknowledge. She even went to the same pub as them, the Ennismore Arms, which stood just at the end of Rutland Mews, and so she may well have known them by sight. And as Lorraine contemplated the public shaming of the young women, it cannot have escaped her that she herself had once stood in their shoes.

And as Lorraine followed Rice-Davies' post-scandal career, she would have found that she had even more in common with her—because Rice-Davies achieved a complete social rehabilitation. She made a series of advantageous marriages and wound up hobnobbing with the likes of Dennis Thatcher, husband of the prime minister. Rice-Davies herself described her life post-scandal as 'one slow descent into respectability'.

We can almost see Lorraine nodding in agreement.

VI

'... THAT LEAVES ME'

that is why education for girls is so important ... if they have a profession or career they can be independent & not a slave to a man & be unhappy

Lorraine Toeg

THE WINTER OF 1962-1963 was England's coldest since the 18th century. It was dubbed 'the Big Freeze', and Lorraine, venturing out to cook for her invalid sister-in-law Dora, noted how carefully Londoners walked around their icy streets. The Big Freeze persuaded Dora she could no longer live in Britain, and she began casting around for warmer alternatives. She settled on Majorca, and Nora allocated Lorraine the family duty of regularly visiting her ailing sister-in-law.

Meanwhile, Lorraine was finding more and more satisfaction in her career. In November 1961, she took a new job as a secretary and librarian at the Royal Central Asian Society (now the Royal Society for Asian Affairs), whose office was in Marleybone, close by where Stephen Ward and Christine Keeler lived. This was the most responsible job Lorraine had ever had and she revelled in its demands, which included keeping up correspondence between the society and universities abroad.

Lorraine got the RCAS job through the Shanghailander mafia:

the Secretary of the Society was a Margaret Marsh, whose father had been the Toeg family doctor in Shanghai. Another of the doctor's daughters had been a beauty and the young Edmund had had a 'crush' on her, but to judge by Lorraine's patronising comments about 'poor Margaret', nature had not been so kind to her. And yet she did not lack for character; during the war she had risen to the rank of Lieutenant-Colonel in Women's Royal Army Corps. Unsurprisingly, her nickname was 'the Colonel' and it sometimes seemed to Lorraine that she never had never laid aside her rank.

The following year Lorraine took another job, with the Army League. This was a think-tank and lobby group headed by General Sir Richard Gale, one of the most senior British Army commanders of the post-war period. She got on very well with Gale; one of the good things she found to say about the disgraced Profumo was that he had supported a push to promote the retired Gale to Field Marshal. For the next two years, she would spend most of her working time toggling between the Army League and the RCAS.

Lorraine had kept up her correspondence with Tokugawa Iemasa throughout the 1950s. Then in early December 1962 he sent her a postcard from a Tokyo hospital, where he was being treated for a heart condition. Speaking of his health, Tokugawa wrote 'good sleep, good food, good behaviour (as usual), good humour (most essential) all combine to bringing out remarkable results'. The gentle, ironical tone was typical of this man who straddled traditional and cosmopolitan worlds. He died ten weeks later, at the age of 78.

Emily was now spending more of her time in New York, but she was still among Lorraine's closest friends. A 1964 letter from

Lorraine recalls their funny, candid correspondence of their earlier days: she gives the news about mutual acquaintances, including a gay couple who invited her to tea parties which remind her of the lavish spreads served up in golden age Shanghai: 'All the best Crown Derby out and silver muffin dishes spread on finest embroidered linen and table groaning with food'. Lorraine kept Emily up to date with news of old Shanghai friends, like the death of Walter Fuchs—the German diplomat from whom the two women had taken language lessons.

And there was more to their mature relationship than just shared memories. Emily had started work on a major new book, a defence of zoos which would be published in 1967 under the title *Animal Gardens*. Emily travelled around the world to gather material for it, including a tour of European zoos on which Lorraine accompanied her as research assistant. Peter Feuchtwanger also passed work her way. For a while the Rumanian pianist Youra Guller was staying in Feuchtwanger's house—she was another Shanghai connection, having lived there in the 1930's—and Lorraine acted as Guller's secretary, a role which brought her into contact with celebrities such as Rudolph Nureyev.

But the most prominent cultural figure with whom Lorraine associated during these years was the writer and painter Anna Kavan. Hailed by Doris Lessing as 'one of the most distinctive twentieth-century novelists', Kavan's reputation went into eclipse after her death before starting to revive in the 2010s.

Lorraine and Kavan were brought together in 1964 by their mutual friend Ann Latch, whom Lorraine met when she was living at *Conygar*. Latch, who had known Kavan since they attended the same boarding school, was concerned about the writer, who was recovering from a suicide attempt. Latch lived in the country and so she asked Lorraine to look in on Kavan, who lived in Kensington, just across Hyde Park from Rutland Mews.

When she first met Kavan, Lorraine was

> *feeling quite overawed and very shy to meet this woman whose books I had read and wondering if I would really be welcome ... Instead of an invalid I saw a woman beautifully groomed, ethereal and so sympathetic to me because I should have taken the trouble to call on her – I loved her from that moment – after that I visited her often ...*

Kavan was a heroin addict and when Lorraine first met her, the writer's overwhelming concern was to secure her supply of the drug. Some doctors in Britain would prescribe heroin to addicts under their care, and Kavan was looking desperately for a sympathetic doctor. Lorraine offered to ask her own GP if they would consider giving Kavan a prescription, but it turned out they were in the unsympathetic camp, and eventually Kavan succeeded in securing a supply through other channels. But like many addicts – and like many addict authors – Kavan was fascinated by the psychology of drug dependency, and when she learned that Lorraine had smoked opium with Emily and Shao Xunmei during her time in Shanghai, she quizzed her closely on why and how she had given up the habit.

Kavan's life had been saturated with trauma. She had been fostered out as a baby, she was fatherless, she made suicidal gestures, and she had inherited from her mother the habit of compulsively lying about her past. One of her circle said of her: 'She lied, she fabricated, she spoke the truth, she was not honest. Where did it begin and where did it end?' Lorraine must surely have recognised a reflection of herself – at least her younger self – in Kavan.

In the last year of the writer's life, 1968, Lorraine saw less of her. The autocratic Kavan ordained that she would receive Lorraine's phone calls at precisely 5 pm – the problem was that by that time of day, she was usually incoherent.

We know about Lorraine's friendship with Kavan because after the writer died, the American scholar Richard Centing considered writing her biography; he asked Emily Hahn for assistance and she put him in touch with Lorraine. In her letters to Centing, Lorraine raved about Kavan but in private, to Emily, she was less complimentary:

> *I found Anna's books very hard to read – she was too sad & masochistic & no humour – at least in her books. I admired her paintings tremendously & love the picture she gave me – though not recognizable really as me … Although* (in Shanghai in the 1930s) *you were working for New Yorker & turning out books while smoking opium your work was never depressing Mickey & your sense of humour never left you – just goes to prove that drugs don't have to make one serious.*

Their shared life in Shanghai was the gold standard against which all else was measured.

Along with work and friends, Lorraine had her family. Since settling in England she had made four return trips home to Australia, but by the 1960s contact with her family was no longer punctuated by long journeys to the other side of the world. As her many nephews and nieces grew up, more and more of them travelled to the UK and her mother Laura visited England twice.

The love/hate relationship between mother and daughter had finally settled into affection, and among the shared interests were the books they talked about in their correspondence. Some of these were old favourites of Lorraine which had been in their Warrawee home when she had been a teenager. One was *The Road to En-dor*, a 1920s best-seller about British and Australian officers escaping from a Turkish POW camp: Lorraine singled this out because Edmund's great friend Geoffrey Fitzgerald was mentioned in it. Others were more recent, like the poet Judith Wright's history *The Generations of Men*—which recalled the fact that Wright, like Lorraine, had attended NEGS school in Armidale. Another was Elspeth Huxley's *Their Shining Eldorado*, which Lorraine described this as 'the best book I've ever read on Australia'.

In Australia, Laura basked in Lorraine's social success. This reflected glory reached a peak with the publication in 1968 of Stanley Jackson's *The Sassoons*, a history of the dynasty which treated Edmund's cousins as quasi-royalty. When the book came out, the *Australian Women's Weekly* serialised it over several issues and Laura wrote from Australia to say how as a result, she had been the centre of attention at her regular morning tea party circle. Her friends were 'almost congratulating your old mother because each one there felt I was somehow connected ... Edmund will be delighted to hear about Australian interest in his family'.

Meanwhile, Lorraine was still constantly circling the idea of moving out of London. For some time she was attracted to the south coast, looking at locations like Hove and Brighton, where Edmund had lived as a teenager. Another possibility was further west at Aldwick, where her good friend Ann Latch owned a pair of cottages; Lorraine hoped she might sell them one of these. In 1966 she made a determined effort to uproot Edmund: the house in Rutland Mews was thoroughly cleaned and repainted, then she got the real estate agents in and put the house on the market. Soon she was writing in terms of 'when' Rutland Mews was sold, but Edmund dug his heels in, and the opportunity to buy the Aldwick cottage, on which she had set her heart, passed. This made her angry. Previously she had regarded Edmund as an oracle, particularly in financial matters; now, she saw the failure to buy Aldwick as proof that he was 'not a businessman'. She no longer looked up to him.

It took a while for her to give up her dream of moving out of London: for some time she even considered moving with Edmund back to Australia, to be closer to Laura and the rest of her family. But the idea foundered on Australia's strict quarantine regulations, which would have prevented them from taking their dog. Edmund refused to budge without him.

To many conservatives, the policies of the first Wilson Labour government seemed like an attack on the very core of English life. Yet these years, 1964 to 1970, have also been dubbed the Golden Age of the British welfare state, a time when the rich got poorer and the poor got richer. Lorraine felt that the world had been turned upside down: garbagemen, she recorded, were making £40 pounds a week. 'Never have we seen such prosperity among working people ... it is retired & middle class people who are badly hit with this inflation'.

By the end of the 1960s, Lorraine and Edmund were certainly finding it harder to manage. They didn't own a car, public transport fares had doubled and shopping was now a major effort as grocery shops had stopped making home deliveries. Even worse, Rutland Mews, for so long the preserve of the comfortable middle classes, was being invaded by newcomers. A member of the pop group The Hollies moved into the street, which deeply impressed Lorraine's visiting nieces but not their aunt: the neighbourhood was now full of 'loud music & noisy parties late at night ... people have made money quickly & then want to have a good address but have no idea how to behave'.

Fortunately, Lorraine had her career to divert her. In 1968 she moved to a new job, a part-time position with The Pakistan Society. Her patron Margaret Marsh was now working as an event organizer and Lorraine supplemented her part-time job by helping Marsh to manage functions for bodies like the Commonwealth, NATO, and government committees. These functions provided her with a stream of anecdotes, for example, about Foreign Secretary George Brown's public drunkenness, but Lorraine's most amusing story from this time is one she told against herself in a letter to Emily.

She had been working as an usher in a Parliament House committee room at a discussion of European Policy in the Middle East. She had been instructed to make sure to seat Israeli officials separately from their Arab counterparts, but ...

> *unfortunately I did not have my glasses with me & got them all hopelessly mixed & there was a lot of trouble & the senior Arab Ambassador walked out with his suite after a quarrel with George Brown, who was in the chair, & Israeli Ambassador & it was all in the papers the next day. The woman in charge was very rude to me & after finishing the rest of the week I left … Margaret Marsh was very loyal & backed me up.*

As her nieces approached adulthood, Lorraine began to see things more from their perspective, and her letters take on a feminist slant. Writing to Emily she commented on Germaine Greer: 'They are growing up in Australia it seems – if any country needs GG it is that one … the wonder is that Australia should ever have produced such a woman'.

In these years, the *Australian Women's Weekly* was the country's biggest selling magazine. It was a major cultural and social influence, and it was passed around amongst Australian women in London. Lorraine was one of these avid readers, but she could be critical of some of *Weekly's* content. She decried the magazine's policy of giving 'all the space to model girls who earn fantastic high money. I wish they would write up girls & young folk ... who achieve things through hard work and study'. In its obsessive coverage of celebrities, she thought, the *Weekly* was 'underestimating the intelligence of Australian women & girls ... anyone would think Hollywood was an Australian suburb'. Reflecting her lifelong reading habits, Lorraine thought the magazine should serialise some of 'the wonderful classics ... the Brontes, Jane Austen, Henry James'.

When Lorraine compared her own life in her twenties with those of the young boomer women around her, she felt they were in a better position. This was certainly true of employment: 'These days a girl with good secretarial experience can always get a good job with adequate wages in any country – not like it used to be when I was young & girls only got a pittance & there was unemployment'. And it was also true when it came to what she described as the 'necessity' of being married, which she had felt so keenly. 'Divorce has not got the stigma it used to have ... better to divorce than stay married & live in misery & unhappiness – that is why education for girls is so important ... if they have a profession or career they can be independent & not a slave to a man & be unhappy'.

By now Lorraine had secured herself just such a role outside marriage. At the end of 1969 she had moved from the Pakistan Society to a new position at the Royal Asiatic Society – a different institution from her earlier employer, the Royal Central Asian

Society. Compared to the previous organisations she had worked for, the RAS had a more serious, scholarly atmosphere: 'I work in Library & Reading Room – that is, helping with cataloguing of new books & periodicals & getting books & journals out for the different professors & readers.' She would stay with the RAS for the whole of her sixties; an experience that she felt validated her life in late middle age. As she commented to Laura:

> *Nothing is more 'soul-destroying' than being in an office & the feeling one is just a cog in a machine, thank goodness I've had interesting work in different Societies – I could never work in a commercial firm. Suppose this is fundamentally because I am a creative type & an artist at heart ...'*

Her attitudes had undergone a revolution. At the age of forty, things had seemed quite simple: marriage to Edmund had brought the material security and social position which were the ingredients for personal fulfillment. This formula had worked for a long time but twenty years later, things looked different. Lorraine now believed that fulfillment lay, not in the role of society matron but in that of an independent working woman. The world had changed, and so had she. Edmund found it more difficult to adjust.

When Lorraine first met Edmund in Shanghai, the Toeg family had been suffused by an aura of wealth and glamour. Now their lives were winding down in a depressing cycle of illness and money worries. In July 1968, Edmund had another stroke, a much more serious one which kept him bedridden for three months. At the same time, Nora was taken ill in Los Angeles and in Majorca, Dora had become housebound. Lorraine became the clearing house for a triangular correspondence between the invalid Toeg siblings, all anxiously enquiring after each other.

Now in his seventies, Edmund was growing curmudgeonly. Even before he fell ill, Lorraine found it awkward having visitors to Rutland Mews, as he tended to just ignore them. And just as he was withdrawing into himself Lorraine, for a variety of reasons – social and financial – was increasingly wanting to accommodate friends, friends-of-friends and family members passing through London; she also took in some of Feuchtwanger's students as boarders. This became a source of friction and when one house guest, a family friend from Australia, outstayed their welcome, Edmund erupted, complaining that he couldn't 'call his house his own anymore' and that Lorraine had turned Rutland Mews into a 'boarding house'. The contrast with his youthful life in the family's 'palace' on Yu Yuen Road must have been painful to contemplate.

This was only part of the story. As Lorraine complained to Laura, Edmund had been

> *getting into such tempers ... He has been like this for years now & is getting worse – he wants no-one in the house for a visit even & when he finds me talking on the telephone to a friend he tries to interrupt me & comes into the room on & off to see if I've finished phone call & if I am still talking utters loud sighs & makes faces ...*

Lorraine kept trying to get Edmund out of the house: on one occasion prodding him into taking a trip to Amsterdam: 'He hasn't been anywhere for years and it took some persuading as he hates leaving his house here'. But then he called the trip off. 'Nothing will induce Edmund to leave this house,' she concluded, 'travel upsets him, and he feels lost without his books

& drawing things around him'. Only one thing could tempt him out of London—a cricket match in Brighton.

Edmund had a reputation as an accomplished painter of racing scenes—Lorraine loyally claimed he was 'recognized as one of the best sporting artists in England'. He could have made money by taking commissions but, again to Lorraine's irritation, he failed to pursue the opportunity. Rather, he was immersed in his daily routine: he would take the dog for a walk in Hyde Park, then catch up with cronies for 'coffee & chat & racing tips ... quite an easy life'. One of these cronies was a retired officer who had been aide-de-camp to the Duke of Windsor during World War II. There was a time when Lorraine would have revelled in this connection with royalty; now it was just irritating proof of Edmund's inertia.

And yet, however much Edmund and Lorraine might have been getting on each other's nerves, that didn't stop them communicating with each other. Lorraine's opportunities to go abroad were now limited, and in May 1970, she leapt at the chance of travelling to the South of France as a paid companion to Edmund's old Shanghailander friend Mimi Compton. During the seven days Lorraine spent on the Cote D'Azur, she and Edmund corresponded every single day. And they still signed themselves Wunsy and Dee Dee.

But now their relationship descended into crisis, triggered by Edmund's growing preoccupation with young girls. A burst of Lorraine's letters to Emily from this period have survived, and from these we learn that 'he has had a new 'Lolita' these past six months & so infatuated that he has become quite mad & treating me like some "old Bag" ... His crazy behaviour has made me feel quite ill ...'

Edmund, she said, had 'been sending quite large sums of money to his Lolita & his complete 24 hour day absorption (*with her has*) really got me down—He talks to himself a lot & I'd overhear imaginary "Love conversations" such as in a loud voice "Oh my darling, one day we will have a riding school together in the country"'. The crowning insult was that the 'Lolita' had been encouraged by Edmund to call him Dee Dee. That was Lorraine's nickname for him; it seemed like she had been replaced. She tried putting her foot down. 'I scared Edmund by getting out my cases, starting to pack, & threatening to return to Mother!' However, some months later she was reporting that the interloper was still calling Edmund Dee Dee but, she gloated savagely, 'in 2 year's time she'll be too old for him'.

Lorraine worried that Edmund might try to act out his Lolita fantasies. But Rose Knox-Peebles, who knew the couple well at this time, saw no evidence to justify these fears. As she says: 'Lorraine was upset that as he got older Edmund began to be keen on little girls and spent money on buying them things like record players—but I thought he was harmless ... he spent a lot of time with our children we never had the slightest feeling he would do anything wrong'.

To make matters worse, Lorraine felt that she had been reduced to the role of a Toeg family servant. In early 1971, Dora had a couple of strokes in succession, and the presence of a family representative in Majorca was deemed essential. Neither Nora or her husband Dan Cromie could leave Los Angeles, Edmund wouldn't stir outside London and so, as Lorraine put it, 'that leaves me'. As she wrote to Emily: 'What a Mother figure I've become ... And there I was in my younger days in search of a Father'.

Then in April 1972 she arranged for a small break for herself, going to Switzerland as companion to Mimi Compton, arranging for a carer to look in on Edmund during her absence. But when Nora found out that Lorraine had had the 'leisure' to go to

Switzerland, she positively 'demanded' that she should also go and visit Dora. Trying to do her duty by both her sisters-in-law, Lorraine told Edmund that when she came back from Switzerland she would go on to Majorca. This prompted another of his eruptions, with him protesting 'how can he be left alone to look after himself, dog & Budgie?'

Torn between the conflicting demands of the three Toeg siblings, she wound up satisfying none of them. Dora died just weeks later.

Now in her early sixties, Lorraine was as active as she had been a decade before. She wanted to travel, she wanted a social life, but instead she was stuck with the needy, grumpy Dee Dee, worrying about money. She must have had a sense that the walls were closing in. And from now on less of Lorraine's correspondence survives; her last surviving letter to Emily is dated June 1972. This had just a flicker of their old edgy, mocking humour which had first sparked in 1826 Avenue Joffre thirty-five years before.

And the mood of her letters to Laura became more and more autumnal. The times were out of joint. She was depressed by demolition of old London buildings, including the former offices of the Royal Central Asian Society where she had worked, and she mourned the end of Sydney's 'dear old clanging trams'. She was dismayed by Britain's accession to the European Economic Community – a forerunner of the EU – noting how as a result, fruit from Commonwealth countries like Australia disappeared from London shops. Edmund was still occasionally venturing out to play golf, but he was increasingly deaf – as was their dog.

Lorraine's consolation was her job in the RAS library, with its 'thousands of old books & manuscripts', where she was now working four days a week. Her satisfaction was crowned in February 1973, when the Queen visited the Society to commemorate its 150th anniversary. Lorraine was presented to the royal visitor: after years of feeling like an outcast and decades of atonement, it was an acknowledgement that she did, after all, belong. The royal benison was bestowed again in August when she and Edmund attended a garden party at Buckingham Palace.

Writing to Laura on the eve of her 64th birthday, Lorraine commented how the IRA's bombing campaign in London had changed the mood in the city. After that, there are no more of her letters surviving for the next ten months, but in the interval Edmund had died at the age of 78.

VII

The Way Home

I did feel flat

Lorraine Toeg to John Murray

Given Edmund's physical and mental decline, his death may have come as a release to Lorraine, but it's hard to say, because from now on the sources for her life dwindle away to almost nothing. The main reason for this was that Laura was herself now suffering from dementia and, no longer able to correspond with her daughter, her collection of Lorraine's letters ceased.

We do know that for the rest of the 1970s Lorraine lived a full and active life. At the Royal Asiatic Society, she was now working as a librarian, and outside the RAS, she continued to take courses and attend lectures. Her nephew David Murray, who visited her in this period, remembers her conducting him around London's great art galleries and museums. Lorraine was now living a life full of art and books.

She maintained her friendships with Margaret Marsh and composer neighbour Peter Feuchtwanger. Alas, Rutland Mews was now suffering another invasion by undesirables, this time by wealthy 'Persians'—Iranians. Once again Lorraine determined to move out, planning to downsize to a flat somewhere. But she never got around to it, and Rutland Mews was destined to remain her home for the whole of her London life.

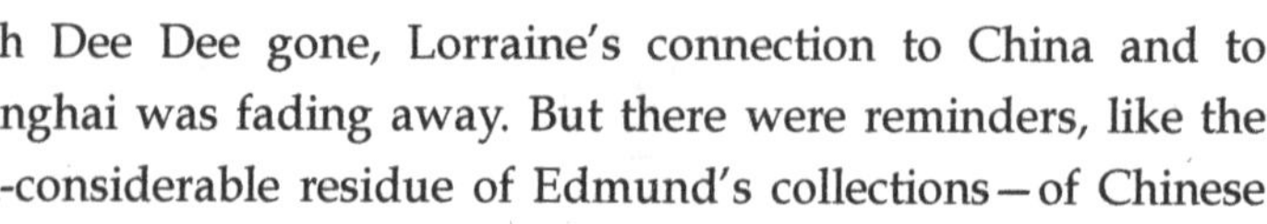

With Dee Dee gone, Lorraine's connection to China and to Shanghai was fading away. But there were reminders, like the still-considerable residue of Edmund's collections – of Chinese objets d'art, Japanese prints, rare books and the like. She gradually began to dispose of these: selling some, giving others to museums.

Another link to the past was her correspondence with Cheng Kuonan, whom she described as 'Edmund's Chinese agent – he looked after Edmund property in Sh'hai for many years, & is a solicitor'. Cheng had escaped from Mainland China in the mid-1960s and settled in Hong Kong, and she remained in touch with him after Edmund's death. He wrote to her on an eclectic mix of subjects including numerology and forward positions in forex trading.

Throughout history, dispossessed émigrés have hoped that a change in circumstances will restore the fortunes they left behind when forced out of their homeland. When Beijing initiated a process of gradual economic liberalisation at the end of the 1970s, Lorraine began to entertain similar hopes, and her letters to Cheng took up the topic. Given the changing circumstances, she wondered, might the Chinese authorities now acknowledge her title, as Edmund's heir, to the Toeg properties in Shanghai which had been nationalised in 1949? Cheng's answer was a polite but categorical 'no'.

It would have been interesting to know more about Cheng. But the truth is that for someone who made so much of her time in China, Lorraine didn't seem particularly interested in its inhabitants. Cheng is one of only a handful of Chinese people mentioned by name in her three hundred surviving letters.

In April 1978 Lorraine's mother Laura died. The family arranged for her to be buried near the grave of Ben Chaffey, the love of her life, who had died forty years before.

After that a few letters from Lorraine to her brother John survive, and in one of these Lorraine describes her job at the RAS:

> *I enjoy my work – am responsible just now for the Exchange Journals & sending out new books to review for RAS quarterly publication – as well as finding books for any reader who comes into the Library. 'Fellows' and members generally know their own way around. But we do get quite a few overseas visitors for research etc. I meet Australians and Indonesians from Australian universities – quite interesting & I am pleasantly surprised at the many new books on all Oriental Subjects written by this new generation of Australian scholars.*

She and John were very much on the same wavelength; in another letter she talks of how the dire warnings of Alexander Solzhenitsyn, the dissident Russian author who had been expelled by Moscow, were being ignored by 'ostrichlike' Westerners who were blind to the Soviet menace. And in May 1979 Lorraine was so elated by the election victory of the Conservative Party under Margaret Thatcher that she rang John in Australia to share the historic news with him.

The following year, Lorraine retired from the Royal Asiatic Society, having worked there for a decade. She felt quite lost without her job, and was delighted when a librarian friend at the British Museum invited her to work there as a volunteer. As she told her brother John, 'I must confess I did feel flat after leaving R.A.S. ... now I've got a rosy future !!!'

But then came disaster.

Towards the end of 1980, Lorraine was walking in a London park when she was struck violently on the head by a soccer ball, which knocked her down. By the eve of her 71st birthday, she had recovered sufficiently to write to her niece Louise Austin:

> *I do get sudden memory lapses as a result of concussion as the ball hit me when kicked not more than 6 ft away and got right temple which bowled me over. Fractured arm, hand, wrist ... I type with left hand and can use index finger of the right.*

A month later she wrote again to Louise, giving the impression she was bouncing back: she talks about exhibitions she had seen—the Bloomsbury Group, Jackson Pollock—and the book she was currently reading, Robyn Davidson's *Tracks*. And for a while it seemed as if she had shrugged off the accident. Charles Boxer got her some work as a research assistant for the Hong Kong author Austin Coates, who was writing a history of European style horse racing in China. In September 1981, Boxer wrote to her about it: 'Dear Wunsy,' he wrote using her time-honoured nickname, 'glad to know you are recovering well'. The following year Emily and Charles visited China, and Emily sent Lorraine a postcard from Beijing. 'I think about you often. We aren't going to Shanghai, though. Too many other places to visit. Love, Mickey.'

This is the last surviving item of their correspondence, forty five years after Emily had, at Edmund's request, thrown a tea party for a young South African woman called Jean who was stranded in Shanghai.

Towards the end of 1984, the Murray family was contacted

by Lorraine's London solicitor. He was concerned that she was increasingly unable to care for herself, and that there was a danger she might be being exploited. Her brother Peter travelled to London and found that the solicitor's fears were well grounded: Rutland Mews was full of cats feasting on choice cuts, while the vegetarian Lorraine was starving herself for economy's sake. Her affairs were in a state of disarray.

Peter sold Rutland Mews, liquidated Lorraine's other assets, and brought her back to Australia. She arrived back in Australia in 1985 and after catching up with family members in Sydney and Nowra, she ultimately moved in with Peter and his wife at The Rock, a village outside Wagga Wagga in the Riverina district of NSW.

Several family members recall Lorraine's arrival back in Australia, it was clear that her condition had deteriorated significantly. She stayed with her niece Gina Oldham, who commented that 'she said so many things but they were so muddled in with other things that I couldn't put any thread to it.' Another niece, Pauline Rayner, who visited her at The Rock, recalls how while her long-term memory—for example, of her time in China, was 'amazing'—she was continually mislaying her personal belongings. It was around this time that according to Emily's daughter Carola, their contact with Lorraine finally ceased: 'We were sad about that'.

Certain ideas began to dominate her thoughts. She became consumed by the idea that her mother Laura had rejected her, that she had 'never loved her'. But there must have been some good times too. At some point in the late 1980s, Hazel Jones came to visit her old friend—like Lorraine, she had come back to spend her last years in Australia. Perhaps she brought back memories of when they had first met in wartime Brisbane, sitting on the steps of the Bulimba hostel in the cool of the evening, raving about Emily's books and planning the wonderful lives they would have once they managed to escape from Australia.

As Lorraine's dementia deepened, life at The Rock became untenable, and she moved into a nursing home in Wagga Wagga. Peter died in 1993, Lorraine died on 7 January 2000, and their commemorative plaques lie side by side in the Wagga Lawn Cemetery.

She clung fiercely to her memories. Among her most treasured possessions was the photograph album which chronicled her life right back to the 1930s. One day in around 1990, Lorraine was sought out by journalist Matt Crosbie, who had heard stories of an extraordinary old lady who had had some colourful connections with the Japanese around the time of World War II. He called on Lorraine at the nursing home, but found it difficult to have a coherent talk with her. He did, however, obtain her permission to photograph the album, and took it outside to get a better light. He noted the photograph of David Niven holding Sammy the boxer dog, and another showing Lorraine in the company of a group of British aristocrats. Crosbie would later recall how, even though Lorraine had given permission and even though it was just a matter of minutes, the nurses had worried that she would miss the album and grow distressed.

Her brother Peter used to take Lorraine on excursions outside the nursing home; she liked going and sitting at the airport, watching planes take off and land. Perhaps the stir of arrival and departure reminded her of her youth, when departure meant escape from boredom or shame, and arrival the prospect of romance. One day a group of Japanese were in the airport and one of them opened a door for Lorraine. She thanked him in his own language, he replied, and to the astonishment of her brother, the largely mute Lorraine burst into Japanese conversation.

Perhaps for one moment Tokugawa Iemasa was ushering her through the door to a golden future.

Acknowledgements

My principal debt is to Lorraine Murray's kin, particularly Louise Austin, David Murray and Pauline Rayner, and including Lorraine Baquie, Susie Disher and Lucy Watts. This book could not have been written without their generous cooperation.

I also owe thanks to:

Sue Wright, who untangled the mystery of the relationship between Lorraine's mother Laura and Ben Chaffey.

Ian Marr, who directed me to David Russell, Doug Hudson and Craig Hudson of Cobar. Their guidance provided the crucial breakthrough which led me to the Murray family.

The archivists of Abbotsleigh School and of New England Girls' School for providing details of Lorraine's education.

Carola Vecchio and Rose Knox-Peebles, with whom Lorraine played at *Conygar* when they were young girls, and who shared their memories of her.

Dr Theodore Ell, who traced Luigi Barzini's travels in China.

Matt Crosbie, who remembered the photo of David Niven and Lorraine's dog Sammy.

Belinda Yuille, Suzanne Kuntz and Michael Duffy, whose readings of the manuscript helped in its development.

And John Minford, without whose help and encouragement this book may never have seen the light of day.

I acknowledge permission to quote:

From the following works by Emily Hahn: *China to Me*, *Miss Jill* and *England to Me*; and from letters by Emily Hahn to Lorraine Murray, courtesy of Carola Vecchio and copyright © the Estate of

Emily Hahn;

From letters exchanged between Lorraine Murray and Emily Hahn, courtesy of Lilly Library, Indiana University, Bloomington, Indiana;

From letters from Lorraine Murray to Laura Glanville, courtesy of Louise Austin;

From postcards collected by Lorraine Murray, courtesy of Pauline Rayner;

From letters from Ella Strom courtesy of the Estate of Ella Viola Brandelius-Ström-Grainger-Manville and the Grainger Museum, University of Melbourne;

From *Nemesis* by Max Hastings, courtesy of HarperCollins Publishers Ltd © Max Hastings 2007.

Quotes from J.G. Ballard from *The Kindness of Women*, London, Harper Collins Publishers, 1991.

Quotes from Dymphna Cusack from *Come in Spinner*, London, William Heinemann Ltd., 1957.

Quotes from George Johnston from *Clean Straw for Nothing*, Collins, London, 1969.

Bibliography

Archival Sources

Indiana University Bloomington, Lilly Library

Emily Hahn Collection: Letters to/from 'Lorraine Toeg', LMC 1438 Boxes 2, 3, 4, 5, 7

National Archives and Records Administration, Washington, D.C.

'Miss Lorraine Murray alias Lorraine Lee': RG 263 Entry A1-2 Shanghai Municipal Police Box 45 #D5695 Murray

National Australian Archives

NAA: A367, C65778 'Russo, Peter et al.'

NAA: A989, 1943/235/1/2/12 Defence – Censorship Timperley, Harold – Activities of

NAA: A4144, 244/1946 'Collaborators – Alan Raymond'

NAA: A6119, 40 'LOCKWOOD, Rupert Volume 1 1939 – 1949'

NAA: A6119, 1256/REFERENCE COPY 'RUSSO, Dr Peter Anthony Vasquez – Volume 1'

NAA: A6126, 62 'RAYMOND, Alan Willoughby (Volume 1)'

NAA: A6126, 63 'RAYMOND, Alan Willoughby (Volume 2)'

NAA: A6202, J 'Petrov Commission: Exhibit J'

NAA: A6335, 39 'Japanese Fifth Column 1941 – 1942'

NAA: B2455, TIMPERLEY HAROLD JOHN

NAA: B2458, 2143151 'RODIE, Arthur Finlayson Douglas'

NAA: BP242/1, Q51424 'Petrov Royal Commission [Royal Commission on Espionage, Commonwealth Police Force, Commonwealth Investigation Service, Queensland'

NAA: C123, 10769 'Sieper (nee Holterhoff), Gerda (Australian of German parents)'

NAA: C320, CIB271'Miss Barbara Davies'

NAA: C329, 457 'Gerda HOLTERHOFF (Objection 85 of 1941; AC)'

NAA: SP1714/1, N51485 'Lorraine Murray'

National Library of Australia, Canberra

NLA MS 9114, f. 1: 'Security and I', transcript of ABC Radio interview by Tim Bowden with Rupert Lockwood 13/7/75, pp 12-14.

University of Melbourne, Grainger Museum

2016/4—Iyemasa Tokugawa Correspondence Unit 1, Copybook Nos. 1-4.

Published works

Alley, Norman, *I Witness*, Wilfred Funk, New York, 1941.

Austin, Louise, *Journey to Tobruk: John Murray – bushman, soldier, survivor*, Pier 9, Sydney, 2009.

Austin, Louise, *Secrets & Silence: A Family Memoir*, Austin Advisory Services Pty Ltd, Sydney, 2003.

Ballard, J.G., *The Kindness of Women*, London, Harper Collins Publishers, 1991.

Barzini, Luigi, *Memories of Mistresses: Reflections from a Life*, New York, Macmillan, 1986.

Bickers, Robert, *Empire Made Me: An Englishman Adrift in Shanghai*, Penguin, London, 2004.

Bickers, Robert, *Out of China: How the Chinese Ended the Era of Western Domination*, Penguin, 2018.

Cusack, Dymphna & James, Florence, *Come in Spinner*, London, William Heinemann Ltd., 1957.

Cuthbertson, Ken, *Nobody Said Not to Go: The Life, Loves, and Adventures of Emily Hahn*, Open Road Media, 2016.

Fahey, John, *Traitors and Spies Espionage and Corruption in High Places in Australia, 1901-50*, Sydney, Allen & Unwin, 2020.

Finch, Percy, *Shanghai and Beyond*, Charles Scribner's Sons, New York, 1953.

Friend, Donald, *The Diaries of Donald Friend*, Volume 1, ed. Anne Gray, National Library of Australia, Canberra, 2001.

Friend, Donald, *The Diaries of Donald Friend*, Volume 2, ed. Paul Hetherington, National Library of Australia, Canberra, 2003.

Grescoe, Taras, *Shanghai Grand: Forbidden Love and International Intrigue on the Eve of the Second World War*, St Martin's Press, New York, 2016.

Hahn, Emily, *China To Me*, The Blakiston Company, Philadelphia, 1944.

Hahn, Emily, *England To Me*, Jonathan Cape, London, 1950.

Hahn, Emily, *Miss Jill*, New York, Doubleday & Company, 1947.

Hahn, Emily, *Miss Jill from Shanghai*, New York, Avon Publishing Co. Ltd., 1950.

Hahn, Emily, *No Hurry to Get Home*, Open Road Media, 2014.

Hahn, Emily, 'Russian-Child's Size', *The New Yorker*, 9 December 1939, pp 52-62.

Harmsen, Peter, *Shanghai 1937: Stalingrad on the Yangtze*, Casemate Publishers, 2013.

Johnston, George, *Clean Straw for Nothing*, Collins, London, 1969.

Manne, Robert, *The Petrov Affair*, Melbourne, Text Publishing, 2004.

Meyer, Maisie J., *From The Rivers of Babylon To The Whangpoo: A Century Of Shephardi Jewish Life in Shanghai*, University Press of America, Inc., Lanham Maryland, 2003.

Mitter, Rana, *China's War with Japan, 1937-1945: The Struggle for Survival*, Penguin Books Ltd, London, 2013. Kindle Edition.

Peh-T'i Wei, Betty, *Shanghai: Crucible of Modern China*, Oxford University Press, Hong Kong, 1995.

Peters, E.W., *Shanghai Policeman*, Earnshaw Books, Hong Kong, 2011.

Price, Ruth, *The Lives of Agnes Smedley*, Oxford University Press, New York, 2005.

Reed, Jeremy, *A Stranger on Earth: The Life and Work of Anna Kavan*, London, Peter Owen Publishers, 2006.

Smith, Bernard, *The Boy Adeodatus: The Portrait of a Lucky Young Bastard*, Melbourne, Penguin Books Australia, 1984.

Schiff, Friedrich, *Maskee - A Shanghai Sketchbook*, [Shanghai?, 1940?].

Springfield, Maurice, *Hunting Opium and other Scents*, Norfolk and Suffolk Publicity, Halesworth, 1966.

Walker, R.B., *Yesterday's News: A History of the Newspaper Press in New South Wales from 1920 to 1945*, Sydney, Sydney University Press, 1980.

Ward, Edward, *Number One Boy*, Michael Joseph, London 1969.

Wasserstein, Bernard, *Secret War in Shanghai*, New York, Houghton Mifflin Company, 1998.

Wright, Sue, *Looking for Laura*, self-published, 2006.

Wrobel, Elinor, *Percy Grainger's 'Nordic Princess': Courtesan and 20th Century Woman*, Catalogue for the Exhibition on Ella Viola Bandelius Strom Grainger, University of Melbourne, 1990.

Wu Zhouliu, *The fig tree : memoirs of a Taiwanese patriot*, Bloomington, AuthorHouse, 2002.

Index

About the Author

Nick Hordern studied history at the University of Sydney before joining the Australian Department of Foreign Affairs. Postings in Pakistan and Sri Lanka were followed by a stint as a political staffer in Canberra. He then moved across to journalism, working for the Australian Financial Review for fifteen years in various positions, including as Senior Writer. In 2013 he left the newspaper to write full-time; his publications include two histories: Sydney Noir: The Golden Years and World War Noir: Sydney's Unpatriotic War, co-authored by Michael Duffy.

www.ingramcontent.com/pod-product-compliance
Ingram Content Group UK Ltd.
Pitfield, Milton Keynes, MK11 3LW, UK
UKHW012253290726
14090UKWH00016B/622

9 789888 843046